Every Tub Sits On Its Own Bottom

The True Story of A Very Unlikely Boy
Who Chose Not To Accept "Reality" As His Destiny.

You can purchase online
@ www.amazon.com or
Now available to Download
www.ardistcooper.com
Email: cooperardist@att.net

By
ARDIST COOPER, JR.

Acknowledgements

I thank my parents for knowingly or unknowingly cultivating my seeds of self-worth and the belief that family is worth holding together—even when you feel that you may never want to see them again on this side of Earth.

I also thank my wife and children, grandchildren, and my great-grandson. Each of you individually and collectively helped me understand myself better by helping me understand others better. On a scale of one to five, where five is the best, you are all a five.

I want to express gratitude to my editor brother, Levon, and his wife, Darlene. Thanks to my brother, James, for stepping forward to help minimize the difficult and exhilarating effort of bringing this book to completion.

To the many people who tolerated me, scolded me, gave me instructions, or supportively observed what was transpiring as I wrote this book, I thank you.

* * *

Additional copies of this book are available
for purchase or download at www.Amazon.com

Contents

Introduction

As a child in Louisiana, I grew up listening to the older folks share years of wisdom by compacting them into short little sayings. I often didn't appreciate these old southern sayings until later in life, when maturity and experience helped me understand the depth of their words.

One such saying is, "Every tub sits on its own bottom." That phrase unknowingly guided and haunted me throughout my life.

Now that I am almost 80 years old, I suppose I'm one of those old folks now. Instead of condensing my life into little sayings, I'd like to share my life story. I'm hoping that, through my story, you understand the wisdom of how every tub sits on its own bottom.

Chapter 1

The Basic Necessities

Growing Up In Warden

I was born Ardist Cooper Jr., on April 15, 1932, the sixth of 13 children born to my parents Arlen and Martha. My maternal grandmother, Maddie (or Grandma), delivered their first seven children (the first two died at birth); the remaining six children were delivered in good health at the county hospital. The whole community, both white and colored folks, knew and respected Grandma Maddie for she was the community's midwife for nearly 60 years. She helped deliver hundreds of children spanning three generations.

I grew up in Warden, Louisiana—a small farming town in Richland Parish. I did not know I was poor—probably because all of the other kids I knew lived as we did. We were sharecroppers, working 15-hour days on a farm owned by The Boss (what we privately called the landowner), scratching out a living and having just enough necessities to survive.

There wasn't much to Warden except a little grocery store, about a mile from our farm, which sold the basics such as dry goods, some work items like gloves and small tools, and a bit of fresh produce. Inside the store was also the town's post office. To our family, buying something from the store was a luxury because we tried to grow all the food we needed.

Sometimes, Mom would give me a nickel, telling me to get a box of salt from the store. I'd run there and back as fast as I could.

When I returned barely able to breathe and dripping with sweat, she would proudly say, "Boy, you was *fast!*"

That always made me feel good, and I ran just as fast the next time she sent me to the store.

Next to the town store was the cotton gin (a machine for separating cottonseeds from the cotton fiber), the scales where we did the weighing, and the barn where we gave The Boss part of our corn and cotton crop every season. In a large pasture behind his store, The Boss kept the mules we borrowed for plowing and hauling. We took the crops to The Boss's scales and got our mail at The Boss's post office. The Boss owned both our house and our farm. He owned just about everything in town except for the corn mill, which all of the surrounding landowners used. That was the extent of the town of Warden.

Sharecropping

As sharecroppers, we worked someone else's land. In exchange for the labor, we kept half of the landowner's cotton and two-thirds of the corn for ourselves. Families were encouraged to have more children because children are your labor force. The more children you have, the more acreage the landowner gave you to farm, and the more money he made. Back then, an average farming family had 10 children. I believe this indoctrination for wanting a large family started back in the plantation days and still stays with our people at some level.

People are born into a sharecropping type of life. My paternal grandfather, Joseph, was a sharecropper and raised his family, with his wife, Dinah, on their boss's land.

As was customary back then, when my father married, Joseph went to the landowner and said, "My son, he need a house."

Then the landowner lent the son a little house on 40 acres of land, two mules for tilling the soil, and a wagon for transporting the crops to the owner's barn. We used part of the 40 acres as grazing pasture for the mules and our livestock. We used a bit of land to build a stable for the mules, then used another portion for a "truck patch"—our personal garden—where we planted sweet potatoes, yams, peas, sugar cane, black-eyed peas, greens, butter beans, tomatoes, and other vegetables. Between our livestock and our truck patch, we always had plenty of food.

One of our most impressive practices was our sound method of storing sweet potatoes and spuds for the year. We built a "tee-pee," a common practice in the South, where we placed a layer of potatoes on the ground, then laid corn stalks over it, then stacked another layer of potatoes, then more corn stalks, and so on, until it grew narrower at the top in the shape of a teepee. We made a 16-inch high dirt wall around the entire base with a small opening. The wall blocked the wind enough to keep the teepee standing all year long. Once a week, one of the children went into the teepee and pulled out the spoiled potatoes. That was all we needed to do to have sweet potatoes from nearly one season to the next one.

As far back as I can remember, Dad used 10 to 15 acres of the farm for cotton. Every year, we harvested 20 bales of cotton; each bale weighed 2,000 pounds. From planting the seeds to picking the cotton, 20 bales took an extraordinary amount of manual labor. Five days a week, we worked from sunup until sundown, pushing through rain, frost, and intense summer heat.

Two to three weeks after planting the cottonseeds, new shoots came out of the ground bearing two leaves each. This meant that we would be picking cotton in two months, so we had better start planting the rest of the acreage with corn, sorghum cane, and ribbon cane. As each of the crops matured, we thinned the fields by pulling weeds and grass to keep them from choking back the yield. We thinned over 30 acres of crops by hand. Even though I was there doing it, it still amazes me how much work we accomplished by hand every day, year after year.

We farmed corn and cotton, which kept us busy for eight months out of the year. During that time, The Boss let us care for his mules and keep them grazing on our pasture. All of the farm equipment—the bridles, plow gear, and everything else—belonged to The Boss. If you owned your own mules or had some of your own equipment, others considered you a slightly higher-level sharecropper. We borrowed everything from The Boss.

For many, sharecropping was a good arrangement. The Boss kept a steady workforce for his land, and we sharecroppers had a home to live in while making a dollar or two a day.

You can't get rich farming this way, but you can survive.

Our Shotgun House

Our house was a typical wooden "shotgun" house common in the South. They called it a shotgun house because each room's door lined up behind the other. Supposedly, if you opened all of the doors, stood at the porch and fired a shotgun through the front door, the pellets would fly clean through the back door without ever hitting anything.

Shotgun homes were usually about 12 feet wide, contained two to three rooms with a kitchen in the back with a door leading outside. It didn't have a hallway, so each room had a door leading to the room behind it.

Our little house had four rooms. You first walk into the living room where a fireplace sat against one wall. The living room was our family gathering area, where we entertained guests, and where my parents slept. They pushed their bed, which acted like a couch when guests came, off to the right side. Behind the living room was a bedroom, another bedroom sat behind that, and the kitchen was all the way in the back. All of the kids piled up between the two bedrooms, two to three of us sharing a single pallet, which was a mattress on the floor.

With a new sister or brother coming like clockwork every couple of years, we usually had at least four to five kids and two adults living in that little house. Surprisingly, I never felt cramped. I loved having my family so close around me. My parents taught us that family is worth holding together, especially in those days, when

4

the size of your family determined how well you survived. With 40 acres to farm by hand, everyone was a vital contributor. Our family was also our safety and support. We looked out for one another, and gave each other encouragement, love, laughter, and hope.

This sense of family and staying together always remained strong in all of us. Years later, fully grown with families of our own, 20 or more of us regularly visited my mother in her little shotgun home. When it was time for bed, no one wanted to stay with nearby relatives. Without much thought, we just pulled out our blankets and lay on any bit of floor we found. Sometimes that meant setting up your blanket on the porch, but we didn't mind so long as we were together with Mom—a family.

To help keep some of the wind out, we plastered the walls with newspaper dipped in a paste made from flour and water. By the grace of God, the paper remained firm throughout most of our winters there; however, I remember one especially severe hailstorm.

The rain and hail came down so hard that it beat up our tin roof and papered walls. We had every pot, container, and cup out for catching water, but we couldn't keep up with the water streaming through our many cracks. The driest place Mom found was right by the front door. She called us all to stand, huddled tightly together, as the deafening hail tried to break apart our house. We stood in that little spot for hours until the storm finally passed.

That storm taught me that no matter how hard life rains down on you, find a dry spot somewhere, and get in it until the storm passes. Life will be all right if you keep looking for that dry spot.

When weekends came, the work didn't stop. Along with regular chores, Saturday was a cleaning day to prepare for Sunday. We broke off tree limbs and tied them together to make a disposable broom. We swept out the house, swept off the porch, and swept under the house since chickens ran around freely all day. We washed the sheets, made the beds, and had everything looking clean and new in time for Sunday.

Part of Saturday cleaning meant cleaning ourselves, too. On Saturday night, we prepared for church by taking our "weekly." One of the children pulled out the old number three. That's what we called the round, metal tub with slightly flared sides. I suppose it was called the number three because it measured three feet in diameter across the bottom. It was just enough for a person to squeeze into for a bath. Another child heated water on the stove and poured it into the tub, and another child added cold water from the well.

In those days, the head of the household washed up first, followed by the eldest boy and so on down the line. The children used a home-remedy soap that Mom made (the store-bought soap was reserved for the grownups). We all shared the same bath water, so the youngest ended up with the coldest and dirtiest water. I don't know if he was any cleaner afterwards, but he had his Saturday bath!

Thinking about the filthy bath water now, I can't understand why we didn't change the water for each person. We pumped our own water, so there was plenty. We had our own wood to heat the water, so there was no cost for gas. Maybe no one wanted to go through the trouble of heating up more water for each bath. We never thought of questioning it back then; it was how everyone bathed in those days.

Our clothes were like everything else about our lives—just the necessities. We all had a set of clothes for work, a set for church, and a set for school. To keep our shoes from wearing out too soon, we ran around barefoot unless we were working, going to school, or going to church. By the time my oldest brother Micah outgrew a pair of shoes and handed them down to the second oldest boy, Caleb, who then finally handed them down to me, the shoes were so worn that the soles would flap loosely every time I took a step. I had to wire the sole to the shoe like a makeshift staple.

My dad had a system of giving us clothes. The family gathered in the living room and he opened up Mr. Sears or Mr. Montgomery Ward's catalog. Then Dad ordered a pair of shoes for this one—"if he gotta have 'em"—or a pair of pants for that one—"if he need 'em." When he finished placing the order, he let us kids look in the catalog.

We all stared at the fancy clothes, the fancy shoes, and the smart looking hats, saying, "Oh, I want *that!*" but we knew we were just wishing.

Dad reminded us, "You ain't got no money to buy any."

Life was simple and difficult at the same time, but I never felt poor because I had everything I needed: a home to sleep in, plenty of food, and a loving family surrounding me.

Hope

In those days, one of the hardest parts about living in the South was the physical and verbal reminders to have no hope. Society kept us in our own schools, our own churches, and our own bathrooms. We had to step off the sidewalk when a white person came by. We maintained a subservient voice whenever a white person spoke to us, always answering, "Yes, sir" or "No, ma'am."

At the store, we had to step to the back of the line whenever a white customer walked in. We constantly feared lynching and tolerated nasty names, and they treated us as though we were barely human.

Despite how difficult life was for colored folks, my parents taught us how to be grateful for everything: for each other, for the clothes on our back, for every bite of food we ate, and especially for whom we were.

I believe this mindset of being grateful for everything—no matter how small—kept me from giving up hope. When I was five years old, I already knew that I wanted something better than growing up and staying on the farm. I didn't know what that "something better" was, but I held so much hope for it, and I knew deep in my soul that I would have it someday. That hope kept me motivated to work for it, no matter how much pain I felt or how exhausted my body became at times.

Years later, my ability to hold tightly onto hope, fueled by the Almighty God, helped me out of the most challenging times of my young life. I witnessed people dying from losing hope while others survived in the same situation. I learned that, when a person gives up hope, they lose their will to live. Hope isn't just a wish or a feeling; it's a powerful motivator, pushing you forward when you can't see much reason to do so.

Chapter 2

Work Training

Plenty to Do

As farmers, there is always plenty of work to do. With such a large family to feed and care for, we all started to contribute very early in life; however, even with all of us helping, my mother still seemed to do more than anyone. She worked the fields with us from sunup to sundown, helped with our lessons, mended our clothes, cooked every meal, managed the house, and kept everything clean. All of us kids helped some, but Mom seemed to do most of it.

Looking back, I really don't know how she did it. To have our breakfast ready every morning, Mom had to get up at least an hour and a half earlier than the rest of us to get the fire started on the stove, knead the biscuits, and fry the meat and eggs. Then, she would wash up and follow us out into the fields when the sun barely glowed enough to guide us. In our tiny wood-burning stove, she'd make enough food for an army within an hour. It was amazing! She did this for three meals a day, day after day, year after year.

My dad had a system for helping around our house. When a child reached three and one-half years old, he took care of the younger children. When I was old enough for that responsibility,

I stayed behind, taking care of the babies while the others left for the fields.

In addition to caring for my siblings, staying behind meant another set of chores. While the others worked in the fields, I washed the dishes, brought in wood for the stove, pumped water for the house, and shelled corn to be ground into cornmeal. I fed the hogs, chickens, ducks, and cows; collected eggs from the hen house; and cleaned the yard in case visitors dropped in during the weekend.

These weren't just chores. These were my lessons for being responsible and learning how to become a provider for my own eventual family. My daily duties taught me how to work hard and make an honest living. I didn't dare think of taking shortcuts or skipping chores because that meant I'd get the strap—or worse— for letting my family down. I'm not sure which I feared more: a beating or their disappointment. With my dad's system, we all learned responsibility very early in life.

As important as I felt with my list of chores, I knew the real expectations came when I turned six. That's when my father decided we were ready for what he called "work training."

Work training meant learning how to work like the adults. I looked forward to it because I missed my family when they all left for the fields every morning. Although we ate together at every meal, I wanted to be next to them all of the time. Working next to them meant I could stay close, and that gave me great comfort.

When I turned six, I became a farmhand, learning how to chop cotton, thin the fields, hook the mules to the plows, plant and harvest vegetables, and pick cotton from sunup until sundown. Whatever the adults did, they expected me to follow.

Teaching and Learning

My father had a different way of teaching. He told you what to do but never explained how to do it. He expected you to learn just by watching and to listen intently to his instructions. Sometimes, he gave us all orders and then watched—like the overseer of the organization. Other times, he sat on the front porch or in the front room studying his Bible. From time to time, he picked up his head to watch us work, then lower it back into the scriptures. To me, Dad was the great leader and my siblings and mother were the teachers.

If he told me to do something I wasn't sure how to do, I'd just say, "Yes, sir!" and run out, acting as if I understood, then secretly ask one of my brothers or sisters for help.

Whether he worked next to us or watched from a distance, none of us kids ever dared asked my father to repeat his instructions or explain how to do something. He had such a stern look about him that we all assumed he wouldn't answer without becoming angry.

Many years later when I was on my own, I told Dad how we children never asked him to explain things because he looked like he'd get angry. When I said this, he seemed slightly hurt.

"Why didn't you just ask and find out?"

By that response, I suspect that we children spent our lifetime missing valuable conversations with our father—all because we were too scared to ask.

Unlike Mom, Dad never joked with us, spoke a kind word of love or praise, or sat around talking. We assumed that he didn't like that type of communication. At the same time, he assumed that we didn't want to be with him. Dad said he used to hear us laughing inside the house; then, as soon as he stepped onto the porch, we suddenly grew as quiet as a mouse. He always wondered why, yet he never asked Mom or any of the children about it.

That was another lesson learned: When in doubt, gather up the courage and ask. Then you'll know for sure.

My father had a commanding way about him. Although he stood six feet tall with broad shoulders and a strong chest, that wasn't what made him so commanding. It was his quiet, deliberate way of speaking. He never hollered or raised his voice. He didn't speak much by way of telling stories or offering casual conversation but, when he did speak, you'd better listen!

When you disobeyed him, he looked you in the eye, quietly said, "Boy, I'm gonna beat you," then walked away.

He never said when he'd do it, but he was a man of his word. When he said he was going to beat you, you would get your beating that day but not know when he'd do it, which was worse. I believe that fearful anticipation was part of our punishment. Dad made it very clear that his word was law. He was very strict about you doing what he told you to do.

I learned that lesson around four or five years old when we were making cane syrup at the mill. When you make syrup, you burn a lot of oak and hickory wood, which burns very hot. As the ashes build up, someone scooped them out into a pile off to the side of the mill. My job was to feed the cane into the mill. When my turn was finished, I carried on with the other children and ran around the mill. Dad was standing around, talking with the other grown folks.

He saw me running around and, in his usual quiet but stern voice, said, "Boy, don't get in them ashes."

I didn't listen and kept hopping my butt around until I accidentally got in those ashes. As usual, I was barefoot and those ashes were *hot*! The soles of my feet were so rough that they didn't burn too badly, but the sides of my feet immediately blistered. No matter how much pain I was in, it didn't soften my dad's heart.

He looked at me, crying and carrying on, and then said in his quiet voice, "I told you not to get in them ashes. I'm gonna whoop you." Then, when we got home that day, he said, "You did not do what I told you to do."

Then he gave me one of the worst whoopings of my life.

Much later, when I was in the military, I realized that whooping taught me more of a lesson than I may ever know. As a soldier, if you're told to do something and don't do it, you could be court marshaled; if you're in a war zone and don't do what you're told, you could be shot or the whole company could be killed. However, as a child, I didn't know Dad was teaching me a lesson. The only thing I thought of was how Dad was the cruelest man in the world. After my whooping, I went back to my room with the other children.

I cried and carried on, asking, "Why does Daddy hate me? I'm a good kid ... and my feet are burned!"

Dad didn't have more than a fourth-grade education, but he was a smart man. He understood human nature and he knew how to figure things out on his own. Maybe that's why he never explained anything to us. He wanted us to develop those same survival skills. Back in those days, you had to make do with what you had, so we learned how to rely on ourselves. I didn't appreciate his teaching style back then, but those keen observation skills and my ability to listen to instruction helped me repeatedly throughout my adult life.

Picking Cotton

When I turned six, I was ready for work training. On my first day out, I proudly strapped on my slightly smaller cotton sack, determined to keep up with the family. I cut my hands quite a bit that day, not sure how to avoid the cotton plants' sharp thorns. It didn't take long before I learned to pick quickly, avoiding most of the thorns.

I worked hard, eager to be as good as my mother, brothers, and sisters. I copied how the others put the cotton into their sack, shaking it down from time to time. Then I followed the adults to The Boss's scales to weigh our bags.

At that time, we called my type of sack a "small sack," which wasn't as big as the full-size one the others used, but that small sack held about as much cotton as I weighed. Dad expected me to pick about 75 to 80 pounds of cotton a day. Sometimes, my mother and sisters put some of their cotton into my bag, so I wouldn't get the strap for falling a little short. This was all serious work and hard for me, but I understood that this was training for the real work.

A full-size cotton sack holds 100 pounds of cotton. I remember that Mom sometimes picked 100 pounds before lunch, and then picked another 80 pounds before sundown. In those days, a good cotton picker could fill a 100-pound sack two to three times a day. Some of my cousins were that good, but my older siblings and mother each averaged 180 to 200 pounds a day, which was still a decent amount.

I always wanted to pick as fast as they did and worked hard, trying to reach that speed, but I didn't stick around long enough to make it. The whole family picked 20 bales of cotton each season. A bale weighed 1,800 to 2,000 pounds, depending on the size of the bale. In the 1940s, we received anywhere from $2.25 to $2.75 per hundred pounds of cotton we picked, working for others to make extra money.

Every time we filled our sack, we took it to the front of the farm for the straw boss (the man who did the landowner's bidding) to weigh. I admit, "straw boss" isn't the nicest name, but that's what we all called them back then. The straw boss could be a colored man, but we knew whose side he was on no matter what color his skin was.

After he weighed our sack, we emptied it into a bigger pile, and then went back out picking until sundown. When our pile reached a full bale, we shoveled it onto The Boss's wagon and took it to his barn for another weighing. After driving the wagon onto the scales, a big vacuum sucked up the cotton, taking it to the cotton gin next door. The gin separated the seeds from the fiber, and then weighed each group separately.

The custom was that The Boss kept half of your seeds as payment for using his land, and then paid for the other half according to that day's market value. Before you received that sum, The Boss took out more money as payment for using his gin. Seeds always paid much less than fiber, but we liked seed because it was "right now money," meaning that we were usually paid before we left the gin.

Receiving payment for our cotton fiber was liken unto the stock market. The Boss may have said that he thought the price of cotton would go up a few cents over the next week or so, and he would sell it when he saw fit—what he called the "right time." Later, we received our share from the sale.

The Boss did not allow us to weigh or sell our own cotton; we had to trust his calculations. Of course, there were times when he cheated us, saying that we only picked 80 pounds when we picked 100, or saying that the bales of cotton sold for $2.25 per pound when it really sold for $2.75, but we couldn't do anything but say, "Yes, sir. Thank ye, sir," and move on.

Thankfully, Dad was an expert manager, so we didn't live paycheck to paycheck, so to speak. Some families weren't as good at managing their money and suffered when The Boss held their cotton for a few days before selling, but we always had the necessities while we waited.

I'm very appreciative of how well Dad managed the family's money and taught us to manage our own money. As an adult, I used that expert money-managing skill to have enough money to send back home and see me through emergencies.

Serious Matters

In those days, the fastest two ways for a colored man to get beat (or more likely killed) were having a white person think you sassed him, meaning you weren't being respectful in your tone or speech, or being accused of looking at a white woman "the wrong way."

One of my dad's younger brothers was killed for sassing his boss. His boss commented that my uncle was taking too long hitching a mule. I don't know exactly what my uncle said back to him or how he said it, but his boss was offended enough to pull out his gun and shoot my uncle without another word. The shot didn't kill him instantly, but his boss wouldn't let him see a doctor to remove the bullet; soon after, my uncle died from gangrene.

My parents never told me this story, but I heard it in the hushed way country folks used to pass on gossip in those days. Some news we didn't say out in the open, but they always managed to pass the story on in a way where, soon, everyone knew about it.

Grown people did not allow children to sit around and listen to discussions about serious matters; however, we usually learned what was going on because our home was small and the walls were thin. We knew that, if we stayed quiet and out of sight, we could linger long enough to hear everything as if we were sitting at the table right next to the grown folks.

If one of us got the nerve to ask questions about the past, the older folks would say, "What do you wanna know for?"

I soon adopted the concept of "what you don't know, you can't speak about."

I recall staring through a crack in the wall one night, watching my dad pace the front room, his mind very troubled. After some time, he told Mom that The Boss short-changed him for his cottonseeds. I don't know what was more frustrating for Dad: knowing that The Boss cheated him or knowing that he couldn't do anything about it.

No man wants to feel powerless, but that incident was a reminder of how powerless we were. Hearing him and Mom talk about this was one of the few times I ever heard Dad express frustration at working so hard, putting up with being pushed down his whole life, and having so little to show for his labors. It was a sentiment that most coloreds felt back then, but we swallowed our bitterness and kept moving on. Saying anything that hinted at unfair treatment or the suggestion of being as good as a white man was liken unto suicide.

Cheating Colored Folks

Innately, I knew I was better than what others told me, but I had nothing to prove it. Society didn't tell me I deserved more; my own folks didn't tell me I deserved more. *I just knew.* I don't know how many times The Boss cheated Dad because they tried to keep that information quiet so the children wouldn't get hot-headed and do something our young minds would feel was justified and regret later.

Cheating colored folks was common practice in those days. That same boss cheated my mother's family out of 40 acres of land they owned outright. Her family was very thrifty. They would go to The Boss's store for groceries, putting the purchases on their account to pay later. Since The Boss wrote down all of their purchases, they had to trust that he recorded everything accurately. Later on, he said they owed more than they could pay back and took their land in exchange. We all knew he was lying because our relatives would only go in for a five-cent box of salt or other small necessities from time to time. They couldn't do anything about it; of course, since The Boss was white, he did not have to answer to any charges of theft.

Back then, colored folks didn't trust white men, but they trusted their own people even less. (I guess it's about the same back then as it is now.) Some colored folks would ask The Boss to keep their money for safekeeping knowing that had its risks too. One time, a colored man came to collect his savings but The Boss and his bookkeeper said they didn't have any of his money and never did. The colored man got so angry, he went straight home, grabbed his gun, returned to the office, and killed The Boss instantly. Then he shot the bookkeeper, who died a little while later. Unbelievably, the man wasn't hanged for the double murder; maybe because he was over 80-years old at the time, maybe not since age seldom mattered back then. Instead, the judge put the colored man in an insane asylum and that's where he died. It was a miracle.

Working Man

For the rest of my work training year, around 1939 and 1940, I continued watching and learning how to farm. When I turned seven years old, my father announced that it was time I took on more duties like the older workers. This included chopping cotton with the adults, then picking it for real—no more practicing. Chopping cotton meant thinning the crop and pulling weeds while the cotton plants were still young. This maximized the amount of cotton produced per row.

My first few days chopping cotton were difficult. I had trouble keeping up with the adults, but Mom and my sister Aaliyah saved me from the strap by chopping some on my row and then chopping their own. By the end of the week, Dad added more responsibilities, but I handled them and kept a decent work pace. I felt like a full-grown farmer.

During cotton-chopping time, some landowners hired outside laborers, and paid children $.50 a day plus dinner if they kept up with the grown folks. Landowners paid grown folks from $.75 to $1 a day plus dinner, depending on the owner. These jobs went fast, so when we heard that someone was looking, we always rushed over, hoping to get the job. When we were blessed enough to get these jobs, we had to walk several miles to the farm, arrive before sunup, and work straight until noon.

During those first six hours, we had one water break, and our only opportunity for a drink was when the water boy came down our row. That happened only three times between sunup and sundown. A lead worker set the work pace and decided when it was time for our water breaks.

In a strong voice, he called out, "*Waaaa-teeerrr!*"

Then, a child, too young to farm (usually less than seven years old), carried over a bucket with cool water straight from the well.

As the water boy continued down the row, another strong voice yelled, "*Waaaa-teeerrr!*" and let the workers know what was coming.

The boy continued down the row, only stopping long enough for each person to put the dipper into that cool bucket and take a full drink. As soon as you took your drink, you went right back to work. Those drinks are still the most refreshing water I can remember. We were so hot and thirsty, after laboring for hours, and that dip of cool, sweet water energized us again. Adults drank first, then the children. We all shared the same dipper, even the white folks overseeing the workers. The water boy moved so fast that all of the workers got their drink within 10 minutes.

Customarily, we had one water break between morning until noon and two more from 1 p.m. until sundown. This was the water schedule everywhere, including families who worked their own farms. Back on our farm, before I was ready for serious work, one of my chores was being the water boy, waiting for my dad's singsong call.

The dinner whistle blew at noon, calling workers to the landowner's house. In case you're not familiar with the old southern ways, we call the morning meal "breakfast," the noon meal "dinner," and the evening meal "supper."

We all sat outside waiting while the maid finished serving the owners inside. Then the maid came outside, passing out pans of food. Everyone received their own pan, about the size of a pie tin, so there was always plenty to eat. We rested for a few minutes, lying on the grass, sitting on stumps or nearby logs, chatting a little and just enjoying our break. At 1 p.m., we walked back to the fields, chopping cotton until sundown.

I was so excited to make my own money that, on my first day, I worked at a feverish pace, trying hard to keep up with the fast-moving adults. I knew that my father wouldn't let me keep all fifty cents of my day's pay, but I figured he'd let me keep ten or fifteen cents. The thought of it made me feel like a rich man! Picturing fifteen cents in my pocket energized me so much that I ended up chopping as much cotton as the adults.

My father was very impressed and asked the person paying if he would pay me seventy-five cents for the day's work since I worked the same amount as a full-grown man. The white man refused and we couldn't argue with him, so my dad let it go. Just having my dad ask made me proud that he thought I was worth a grown man's pay.

Before the season ended, we did some day work for another farm owner. I worked just as hard, keeping up with the adults. This time though, the landowner paid me seventy-five cenets for the day. My father let me keep an entire twenty-five cents! I was only seven years old with twenty-five cents in my pocket. I felt so wealthy and grown up.

When cotton-chopping season ended, we returned to our farm where plenty of work waited. While we thinned the corn and tended our truck patch, I watched the cotton mature with dread because I worried that I couldn't pick cotton fast enough now that the adults expected me to keep pace with them. For two months, I went about my chores while keeping an eye on the cotton bushes. I became more fearful as cotton-picking time came closer.

Chapter 3

Keeping Up

The Real Work

The day finally came when I stopped practicing and started to do real work. I was seven years old, which meant that it was time I strapped on a full-size cotton bag, picking cotton with the others from sunup to sundown. Although Dad didn't expect me to fill it, he did expect me to come close. I cinched that sack on as tightly as I could. The sack was so big that it dragged behind me as I tried to keep pace with the rest of the family.

From Monday to Friday, we marched out into the fields a little before sunup. We wanted to get as much done before noon because the dew was still on the cotton, which added a little more weight. When it got too hot, the cotton got lighter. Besides, it got so darn hot that you wanted to work as hard as you could before dinner because it was hard to pick at that same speed in the heat. Usually, we filled our first bag for weighing around 11 a.m., then kept picking until dinnertime. By the time I was eight, I picked 160 pounds of cotton each day.

We knew the time of day by watching our shadows. I always kept close watch over my shadow because the closer your shadow got to you, the closer it was to noon and to hearing the lead in charge (who was Dad on our farm) shout our favorite words.

"Okay, dinnertime!"

You could also tell how late it was by seeing how far your shadow stretched from you. The further it was, the sooner it was to supper and the end of a very long day.

Mom weighed her first bag a little earlier than the rest so she could make dinner for us by noon. Our family always ate every meal together. At 1 p.m., we filed back out to the hot fields and picked cotton under that scorching sun until sundown. It amazes me how much torture the human body can endure. Men, women, and children, soaked with sweat, bent over double as they hustled through the fields, picking for 15 to 16 hours each day.

Cotton-picking season lasted three months. I don't know how we managed to keep up the pace all day long without passing out from heat exhaustion and dehydration. Even in our own fields, we never carried water; we just waited for our customary water-boy schedule: just three stops for water to last the entire day and nothing but a straw hat for protection. Somehow, we got used to working that way. Like everything else back then, we never questioned or thought of changing it. We just accepted it.

My dad demanded extreme efficiency and high production. If we ever dared slack off or play during work time, we'd get a whooping. That happened to me when the school had their annual fundraiser to raise "4-H Money." I don't know what the 4-H stood for, it just was what we called it. To raise 4-H money, the schoolchildren volunteered to pick cotton all day on someone else's farm. The money earned from that cotton went directly to the school. When the teacher sent us out to pick cotton, I played more than picked, and ended up with maybe 25 pounds of cotton, if that.

She told my dad that night and I got one of the worst whoopings of my life. Dad usually never explained why he was going to whoop you before he did, but this time he had something to say.

In his quiet, stern voice he said, "I didn't make you go. I didn't tell you that you had to go pick no cotton for the school. You volunteered after Ms. Lara asked you. You went out there and you played around. You don't do that. You don't go on nobody's job and play. If you go, you work."

I can't remember if he used the switch or the strap (a thick piece of leather used for sharpening razors), but I remember hurting for days. That strap always hung by the fireplace and was his favorite tool for whooping. Boy, let me tell you, I was about eight years old at that time and that lesson left such an impression on me that I never played on a job again.

Even when I was grown up and worked for the union, people would say, "Man, you don't have to work like that!"

I would always answer, "The man hired me and all I'm supposed to do is work eight hours a day, so I'm goin' to give him a full day's work."

What I did then was hard work, but it wasn't as hard as farming or other jobs I had afterward. Working at full speed for eight hours a day didn't bother me. That tanning on my fanny years ago taught me integrity in my word and pride in my work.

My Mother's Hum

Much like her own mother, Mom was very loving and had more patience than Jobe. No matter how tired she was or how demanding we children were, she never raised her voice and kept a patient, loving way about her. As hard as she worked, I never heard her complain and always kept her gentle spirit.

I remember her always humming, just stopping long enough to answer our questions or give us an order, then pick up where she left off. Mom could be trouble-hearted, but she still had that hum in her. I suspect that the humming helped ease her mind and kept her company.

My mother always hummed the old gospel, "Ain't Gonna Let Nobody Turn Me Around." The lyrics went something like this:

Ain't gonna let nobody turn me around
Turn me around, turn me around
Ain't gonna let nobody turn me around
I'm gonna keep on a-walkin', keep on a-talkin'

Marchin' down to freedom land

Ain't gonna let segregation turn me around
Turn me around, turn me around
Ain't gonna let segregation turn me around
I'm gonna keep on a-walkin', keep on a-talkin'
Marchin' up to freedom land

When I was a child, I loved listening to my mother hum. Her music somehow filled me with hope and peace. I used to sit underneath an old fig tree, just outside our kitchen window, and listen to her hum in the kitchen as she prepared our meals. Sitting in the shade, hearing my mother hum like that, you'd think the world was sweet everywhere. Life felt so beautiful at that moment, I often sat there and cried—not from sadness, but because it filled my heart with so much joy. In hindsight, I realize that Mom is the queen of my success.

Maddie and Marlon

My maternal grandmother, Maddie, lived on the "next 40," meaning another 40-acre farm. Back then, we considered five miles an easy walking distance. One mile was nothing because I could easily run all the way to the store and back, which was only a mile from home, so having Grandma live on the next 40 felt very close. Her children and stepchildren and my brothers and sisters played back and forth at each other's houses.

Even when she had all 12 kids running around and bothering her, asking for this or that, she always remained patient, never hollered, and never said no. Back then, folks always kept food out in the kitchen.

All day long, one of the children would ask, "Grandma, can we have some bread?" or whatever was within sight.

Even if we were close to eating up all her bread, she always said yes.

Grandma had this spirit, which looked like joy in her heart. All of the children—and all the adults who ever met her—thought

24

she had the best personality. Most of the older folks back then hummed a good deal and Grandma was no exception. She was always doing what the older folks called "making melody in their heart."

Now that I'm nearly 80 years old, I find myself humming a good deal, too. It distracts your mind from what you're thinking about and sometimes it's the best way to stop worrying. In our reading of scripture, Ephesians 5:19 tells us, "Speaking to your-selves in psalms and hymns and spiritual songs, singing and mak-ing melody in your heart to the Lord." In other words, you get the full chance and have the ability to encourage yourself. You don't actually need anyone to encourage you. It is an innately created ability. The older folks seemed to know that with their humming. They understood how to encourage themselves no matter how dif-ficult their challenges.

Before Grandma's time ended on earth (somewhere between the age of 93 and 100), I enjoyed some happy days and nights in her house. Even as I ran in and out of the house playing with the other family children, I could always hear her laughter as the grown people talked. When I was around Grandma, I felt light and carefree. Everything always felt right in the world.

Tragedy Strikes

Sadly, tragedy hit Grandma's family a few years later. Her daughter, Alva Lee, fled with her three children to Grandma's house. She had done that several times before when her husband was abusing her, but he could usually convince her to go back home. This time, no matter how he pleaded for her to come back, she refused.

One evening, right before sundown, Alva Lee's husband hid inside Grandma's house with a gun, waiting for his wife to come home. When the door opened, he shot twice, killing Alva Lee and shooting Grandma in the face. He shot himself after that, but it wasn't serious and he healed in a couple of months. He served three to five years for the murder. When the prison released him, no one heard from him again.

When the news spread of this tragedy, it was as if ice water had poured down all over the community. It was the first incident of this kind in our area of the country. Sadness hung over the town for a very long time, and many sent prayers to God for comfort. Grandma recovered from the gunshot, but she carried the pain and disfigurement for the rest of her life. The doctors didn't know what to do with that type of wound, so they left the bullet in her face, leaving her to heal as best as she could.

Grandma's first husband (my mom's dad) died before I was born, so I grew up knowing Grandma's second husband, Marlon. We children loved him for his gentleness and kindness, and especially for one of his specialties—cooking community barbecue on the Fourth of July. For the Fourth, it was customary for one of the landowners to give a goat to the community's colored folks. The whole community looked forward to this great event, especially the children. As a child, all food set before you was good.

The Pastor

By the time I was born, my dad was a full-time pastor. Although his reading and writing abilities were limited, he was a powerful orator. He spoke so boldly about salvation and damnation, quoting from scripture with such knowledge and explaining it with such charisma, I always felt excited, no matter how many times I heard it before. It was amazing to hear my father's usually quiet voice transform with such force and emotion. His words boomed effortlessly, filling the whole church with his pride in Jesus Christ and faith in God. Most times, church service seemed long for an energetic boy my age but, when my father spoke, all of my restlessness fell away as I listened, feeling my soul uplifted.

During Sunday service, I especially loved the singing. In those days, the congregational singing was similar to the post-war gospel quartet Five Blind Boys of Mississippi. Everyone sang together, overflowing the small church with all of their passion and belief. The old hymns stirred my soul, inspired me, and gave me hope. It was powerful sitting there, listening to the entire congregation

singing, "Father I stretch my hand, to thee no other help I know
..."

I didn't hear Dad preach every Sunday; he and Mom often walked to other nearby churches where he preached by invitation. Then, my grandmother would walk all of us kids down the dusty dirt road to our "home church," which was the closest church to our home and the community church. Since then, I have met many a charismatic preacher, but few inspire me as powerfully as my father did.

Chapter 4

School

The Little Schoolhouse

As farmers, we only went to school during the "off-season"—November through February, when the fields lay fallow waiting for spring seeding. We usually pulled all the cotton and corn by Thanksgiving; however, sometimes we had a "scrap" bale of cotton right before Thanksgiving, which was a light bale of 1,200 to 1,500 pounds.

Getting a scrap bale was a good thing because it meant that "you is gonna have a real good time for Thanksgiving!" as we used to say.

During the off-season, we still worked every day doing our serious chores, but they were nothing like farm work because you didn't have to pick cotton, pull corn, or dig potatoes. For me, the off-season meant school, which I hated.

Every morning, rain or shine, we walked the two-mile dirt road connecting our farm to the little schoolhouse, which taught colored children from primary to eighth grade. Unlike today, our primary school had children ranging from six years old to teenagers.

As farmers, we started attending school when we could, and sometimes not until we were seven or eight years old. There were times when you had to skip a year, depending on whether they could spare you on the farm. I was 11 years old in the fourth grade and wasn't considered behind in school.

In hindsight, I believe we made a mistake when we later integrated the schools. We thought integration was good—and it was good to a great degree—but we lost many of our fine teachers when we integrated. When our teachers were only teaching colored folks, they could teach right out of high school without a college degree. At 18 or 19 years old, they were still good. When we integrated the schools, we lost most of those good teachers. In our school, only one or two teachers could go on teaching. One was the principal; the rest of them probably went back to farming.

My second-grade teacher lives around the corner from me now in San Francisco. I ran into her one day when I was visiting the church not too far from home, and there she was. We looked at each other with such surprise. Fifty-three years later, we ended up neighbors—over 2,000 miles away from the last place we were neighbors.

In our little schoolhouse, we had a full day of learning, starting at 8 a.m. and ending at 3:30 p.m. for the younger kids; older children stayed until 4:30 p.m. Despite the various age differences among all of the kids, we rarely had any trouble. No one dared pick on someone else because they usually had an older brother or sister nearby, and the teachers were so strict that we should have called them wardens instead of teachers.

After eighth grade, many stopped going to school because the closest high school was 10 miles away. One of the white schools donated an old bus to our community, but we could hardly get it running. Most kids couldn't go to high school every day unless they started walking very early in the morning. Since very few of us had mules and hardly anyone had a wagon, our feet were the most reliable way to travel.

Good and Bad Times in School

School was tough for me. No matter how hard I studied, I always struggled with some subjects and the worst was spelling. Children can be cruel, and they teased me mercilessly for missing my spelling lessons. The girls were the cruelest because they were always the best spellers in class. To this day, I sincerely believe that girls naturally spell better than boys do.

Every week, we studied our spellers, which contained the words we needed to learn by our Friday exam. On Fridays, the teacher lined us all up in a row, shoulder to shoulder, facing her. Then she walked down the row, stopping in front of each child long enough to say a word from the speller. If we didn't spell it correctly, we opened our hand, palm facing upwards, and *whack*—she came down on you with a ruler. Many rulers hit my palms in those days.

My teachers were very strict. They made sure the parents re-inforced your learning. Whenever I missed my spelling word, my parents knew. Honestly, I don't know what was worse: being pun-ished in front of my classmates and teased, or having to face my dad's anger from not doing well on my lessons.

Dad made sure we learned our lessons every week. He had this way of asking questions to check if we knew our lessons, even if he never read them himself. When he called you up to recite your lesson, boy, you'd better know it! Mom helped us study, reviewing lessons and quizzing us, and was always a patient teacher. One of my most challenging times was learning my numbers. No matter how hard I studied, I just couldn't count from one to a hundred.

One night, my father stood me by the little fireplace in the front room and said in his quiet, authoritative way, "Boy, you better learn how to count from one to a hundred."

I was about nine years old at the time and knew the meaning in his voice. It wasn't a suggestion or a wish; he was giving me an order. I stood there, reviewing numbers with him, my mind com-pletely blank after the number five. We started over and I was stuck in my twenties and thirties. The more he kept trying to make me learn, the more frightened I became and the more I messed up on the numbers.

After a while, he sat back, frustrated, and said, "Boy, you get *outta* here! When I get you back in here, you better know how to *count!*"

I knew I had a couple of days before he called me back in, but just from him drilling me and all of Mom' s reviewing, I knew I had the numbers inside me—they just couldn't come out for some reason. When Dad sent me off that night, I was so scared that I ran straight into the back room and counted from one to a hundred so fast! The numbers came spilling out almost faster than I could say them. I knew I could count and I did it perfectly. *I was good!*

School was difficult for me and I dreaded every day of it, but I thank God now for the strict teachers and the parents who saw to it that their children followed the rules. Although I certainly didn't feel it at the time, I am grateful for them. I only attended school up to the fourth grade, but I received a solid block of learning that carried me as an adult through some very difficult times.

What I liked most about school was meeting all of the other children from miles away. When the weather allowed, we played basketball, softball, or marbles. I loved marbles and always wanted to play, but I hardly ever did. The problem was that kids shot marbles for keeps and I wasn't any good at shooting, so I always lost all of my marbles. It cost a nickel to get another bag of 10 marbles at the store, and I didn't have a nickel.

I loved meeting the other kids, but bitterness came with that sweetness. I had to contend with some of the children calling me names. They teased the texture of my hair and the darkness of my skin. We were all colored but, even among colored folks, we had a type of hierarchy where we considered lighter-skinned—what we called "high yellow"—folks better than darker-skinned ones. Because whites indoctrinated us with the idea that they were better than coloreds, our own people judged and turned on each other based on skin tone.

The "N" Word

This concept is one of the most depressing and hurtful experiences I witnessed throughout my life—especially these days when black folks call each other the "N" word, meaning "nigger." I just don't understand it. I've heard that nasty name all my life, and I fought so others would see me as a fellow human – if not an equal, then at least someone who deserves respect. To hear our own people casually use that vile name on each other hurts me more than I can say. I try to educate those who use that word because it's a lowdown, dirty shame. I speak to many individuals about it and they mock me, which shows how they've lost respect.

"You use that word as a joke to one another. How would you feel if a white person come up and called you that?"

They puff out their chest, get upset, and say, "Oh, I wouldn't take it!"

I explain, "Then how can you call one another that? The word has the same meaning in the dictionary whether you say it or a white person say it. It carries the same meaning of deteriorating your worth. When you say it, you also talkin' about yourself. Too many folks have died for you to use that word so loosely. You better than that."

They don't listen. They call me an old man among other things. I learned to accept it because I can't stop it, but it just burns me up. I keep hoping that at least one out of 10 people may listen. They might not stop saying the word now, but hopefully they'll stop later.

When the children at school teased me for being darker than they were, I believe it was the same reason that white men talked down to us. At some time in our lives, we humans create a need to feel better than or better off than others. When the white man treated us as if we were less than human, and pushed us down, he needed to do that to feel good about himself. I think the colored children at school needed to tease the other children with darker skin or nappier hair to feel better about themselves.

This human need to feel superior showed up everywhere in my life. When I was a child, it was widely practiced in colored society to rank people according to how much they had and how they looked. A plantation worker was less than a sharecropper, a share-cropper with no mules was less than a sharecropper with mules, and a landowner was better than everyone else. Even in my family, when we children antagonized each other, we called each other "black."

When my mom heard that, she asked, "Now, how can a kettle call a pot black?"

We knew she was right, but we wanted to feel superior some-how, even if it meant we were insulting ourselves, too.

Chapter 5

Turning Points

Uncle Charles and the KKK

As if Aunt Alva Lee's murder and Grandma's shooting weren't enough to keep the family in mourning for the rest of our lives, another tragedy struck our family. My dad got word that his youngest brother, Charles, was on the run from his white masters, the Ku Klux Klan.

We heard that Uncle Charles refused to do something ordered by his boss, but no one knew what that was. In those days, a colored man refusing a white man was enough reason to be killed. On the night we heard about Uncle Charles, we kept the house dark for fear the KKK was watching our house and thinking that Uncle Charles would try to make contact with Dad.

I remember all of the children sitting in our room, anxiously huddled together in the dark and waiting for something to happen but afraid of what might happen next. We sat there all night, listening to the crickets outside and Dad pacing back and forth across the floor, too worried to stay still. After many long hours, I got tired and nodded off a few times but, as soon as I heard a little noise, I jumped awake, imagining that someone was coming in to hurt us.

Then, late in the night, a man came to our door and talked to Dad for 15 or 20 minutes. I couldn't hear what the man said but, after he left, Dad remained quiet for a long time. Then I heard Dad tell Mom that the man said he knew where Uncle Charles was hiding and Uncle Charles asked Dad to go to him with some clothing.

Dad was so torn. I could hear him crying in the next room, telling Mom he didn't trust that man and believed it was a trick. Dad suspected the KKK had that man lie and hoped that Dad would lead them to his brother. Whether he could lead them or not, they'd kill Dad that night and Uncle Charles when they found him. That much we were certain.

However, there was a very small chance that the man was speaking the truth. Dad knew he was possibly deserting his brother when he needed him the most. Whatever Dad decided, it seemed as if Uncle Charles was doomed to the same fate. Once again, I saw my strong, proud father have to accept the bitterness of being powerless.

We continued sitting in the darkness, not daring to say a word. The only sound was Dad quietly crying from guilt and frustration for his brother. His tears and pacing continued until the morning. Without saying it, we all knew that Uncle Charles's chances of escaping the KKK disappeared with the darkness.

For more years than I can count, we held onto the hope that Uncle Charles did get away that night. We expected him to show up alive some place, sending word to his mother or brother that he made it to safety. This type of hope, during times of extreme darkness when slavery separated families, likely birthed an old slave song we all knew: "Keep your lamp burning in the window until your son comes home."

No matter how desperate a situation was, we were taught, "Keep hoping." Hope keeps you alive.

Ever since that tragic night, my grandmother hummed the same songs as she worked around the house and farm all day, but her humming seemed different. It sounded as if she was saying goodbye to her son forever. I don't know how I knew; I just knew.

We never heard from Uncle Charles again. Many years passed before our family finally accepted he was gone. We strongly believed, with his family nurturing and strong relationships, that if he did make it to safety over my grandmother or my father's lifetime, he would have sent word.

I believe that my dad spent his whole life haunted by his decision not to go to Uncle Charles that night. Whether or not that person in the darkness spoke the truth, we would never know. It was a tedious decision for my father to make, but I believe he made a sound choice.

Pearl Harbor

Despite the cruelty of slavery ever present, promoted by this country's laws and powers—Sweet Land of Liberty, Justice for All, and In God We Trust—we, a nation of rainbow colors, heard the prayers and cries for freedom.

On December 7, 1941, the cosmic world turned upside down. The Imperial Japanese Navy conducted a surprise military strike against the United States naval base at Pearl Harbor, Hawaii. We were moving fast into World War II. Although no one had electricity in the backcountry, news about the war spread fast through the farms.

Both white and colored folks felt as if the country would be lost, and feared that the Japanese would take over our land and make coloreds and whites their slaves. Having this common fear united us slightly. At that time, I noticed that the whites talked to us a little better—not all friendly and equal, but a little better. White men, who never gave you the time of day, would hang around fences for a few seconds to talk about the latest war news. Attitudes were shifting ever so slightly, but they were shifting.

After the bombing at Pearl Harbor, rumors spread that, if you were warm, the draft would get you. The farm owners united very quickly, trying to convince the draft board that one man per family had to stay behind to farm and provide food supplies for the war.

This slowed the draft from taking all of the men, but most of them eventually had to go.

In the beginning of the war, colored folks were especially scared because the white men told us that they took the colored men first, put them on the front line, and the white men followed behind. We all believed that, once drafted, we would probably never return. Still, many colored men signed up to fight before their draft letters came.

No matter how badly we were treated, we still had a strong love for our country. I believe it was because America was the only country we knew, and we didn't know any better treatment. America was our home and we wanted to defend it. I guess it's like your home life. No matter how bad it is, it's home.

Our war news came from the white man. We didn't know how to read papers and only knew one colored man, living one-quarter mile away, who owned a battery-operated radio. Of course, we believed whatever the white men told us because they were white, and they didn't waste any time scaring us:

"If you guys think you're treated badly now, you wait until the Japanese take over this country! You're gonna be their slave and it'll be much worse!"

That type of propaganda continued for a long time. When the white men returned from fighting, they scared us more by telling stories of how the Japanese treated the colored men worse than the whites treated us. Of course, they made up the stories, but to us it was the truth ... and we were scared! I think they made up these stories because the white man was worried about losing us. If we all volunteered to fight, the landowners would lose their workforce, which meant they'd lose their farms.

Much later in the war, we learned that the army did not send colored men to the front lines at all. When they came back from fighting and told us the real stories, they said that the army kept coloreds back, doing menial, heavy labor. Coloreds fought in segregated armies and the whites widely believed that colored weren't smart enough to fight. They still treated us like the Dred Scott days of the 1800s, where they considered a colored man one-fifth of a person.

The white men didn't realize that they didn't teach us anything except how to be a farmer, so we didn't know how to do anything else. It wasn't because we weren't smart enough. It was because we never had the opportunity to learn. For generations, no one taught us to think.

Opportunities and Hope

With the men gone, women soon took over areas of farming they never touched before, and they did a fine job. Women drove heavy-duty trucks, worked in factories, and kept our country running. Soon, children under 18 years old started to do jobs left by men. Those men not drafted had their pick of available women, and we called these players "jodies." Young or old, we called any man not eligible for the draft a "4F."

Although the war brought great sadness, with large numbers of troops killed, it also brought new opportunities that may have never been possible otherwise. By the middle of 1942, shipyards all over the country started calling for more workers. Without education or experience, they would hire a man just for showing up. The shipyards paid more in one day than what a farmhand made in a year. Many 4F farmhands, both white and colored, deserted the fields for promises of an easier life and more money. The radio kept playing ads "Go west, young man!" These ads lured 4Fs to Chicago, New York, Detroit, and California. Everything sounded so much brighter with lots of fun, games, and endless good times.

The colored workers relied on each other to get out of the farm. When one person got a job and a place to stay in the city, he reached out to his family, letting them notify other family members, friends, or neighbors that they could stay with him until they were established. This is how huge numbers of colored folks left the oppressive farm life and migrated to the cities.

Once in the cities, the exciting good life, seen for the first time, seemed lavish in comparison to how they lived back home. They felt freed from their slave master's hand and lived as if there were no tomorrow. Families and friends left behind on the farms felt the hand of slavery loosen and started to enjoy their lives more, too.

For the first time, coloreds felt they could escape their hardship once they got word from their connection in the city. Even though they still worked hard on the farm, coloreds were feeling a little freer. They felt hope. They believed that freedom was theirs this time. The war gave coloreds an opportunity to get good-paying jobs without any formal schooling beyond their usual third- or fourth-grade education. As terrible as the war was, with its tremendous death toll, it was our only chance to live better.

I'm not saying that the war was good. I definitely do not support the Japanese attacking Pearl Harbor. I believe those stiff-necked, cold-blooded people provoked God, who creates everything. The war wasn't the answer to all of our racial prejudices and cultural divisions at that time, but I firmly believe that the war changed the dynamics of how all Americans had to interact with each other. Because of this, it brought renewed hope for coloreds.

Plowboys and the Draft

As the war continued with such brutality, we didn't know if our country was going to survive. My father escaped the draft because he had six dependents at that time. My oldest brother, Micah, received his draft notice along with most of the men in his age group. When he got that dreaded "Greetings from the President" draft letter, it felt as if the stars fell out of the sky. My parents held that letter, crying and carrying on. Then we children started crying, not really knowing why we were crying, but crying with all the sadness we felt around us.

Before Micah left, he was the chief plowboy. My dad wasn't on the fields working like he used to because he was busy preaching and visiting. Before sunup, he told us what to do for the day, and then checked our work at the end of the day. Micah was in charge, making sure we all walked the chalk line, doing the expected jobs at the expected speed. When Micah left for the war, we felt a strange hole in the family—not only because he was the first to leave the family, but because he was our leader and ran the farm. With him gone, we had to adjust to a new supervisor and one less person to help with the massive workload.

Our new supervisor was the second oldest boy, Caleb. When Caleb became number one plowboy, it meant that I came up the line as number two. I was nine years old but feeling twenty-one in maturity. My family expected more and more of me on the farm, and I felt more nervous and scared with each new expectation. I knew it wouldn't take long before Caleb also got his draft notice. Although I had older sisters who could handle the plowing, Dad held two strict rules: Boys never did the dishes and girls never plowed. That meant I'd be number one plowboy soon, and I dreaded it.

In 1943, Caleb got his "Greetings from the President" letter. My parents were full of fear, doing everything to defer his draft. Every day, we heard about more planes shot down, another ship sunk by torpedoes, and a new list of men killed. The rising death toll sunk our hearts. America was so deep in the war that we couldn't see any end in sight. All we could be sure of was how scared we were that Micah and Caleb would never return.

When Caleb's draft letter came, I was scared for him and for myself. I was only 11 years old and didn't know how I'd take on the responsibility as head of the farm. I knew how to endure the sun-up-to-sundown work schedule, but all of the responsibility and ex-pectations scared me beyond explanation. I knew that Caleb had 10 to 20 days before he shipped out. During that time, I went crazy trying to think of all the ways he could stay. I hoped that he failed his physical examination, but he passed. The Boss and my dad were scared too. They tried to do what they could to defer Caleb's draft. With no way out, Caleb planned to leave in a few days.

Adding to my fear, my father—a tough and very exacting man—would walk down a row and, boy, it had better be perfectly straight and evenly spaced from the other rows! If it wasn't, you were going to get a beating and have to plow the whole field all over again. I don't know what I feared most: the whooping or my dad's dis-appointment. To tell the truth, I don't know if my dad would've whooped me for not plowing right. I let myself imagine the worst, and a frightened child's imagination can be worse than any reality.

Chapter 6

Running Away

A Spontaneous Decision

Much of my fear about becoming chief plowboy was due to a lack of belief in myself, regardless of how much my mother encouraged me. She was always so good about praising us and helping us feel good about ourselves. When I caught a small fish and showed it to her, she would get all excited and say, "My! Look how *big* that is!"

Her praises felt good, but they didn't raise my belief in myself. No matter how much encouragement she gave me, I wasn't equipped to accept it, so I remained insecure. I wasn't yet 12 years old, and I knew Caleb was days away from being drafted. I was so nervous about becoming chief plowboy that I decided my only solution was to run away.

I woke up without thinking about leaving. I worked all day like any other day, not thinking about leaving. Then, at sundown, as everyone walked back to the house for the night, something clicked inside me. I suddenly felt a strong, spontaneous urge to leave right away.

Without questioning my actions, I grabbed my coat and hid it behind the barn. Everyone was busy with evening chores while

Mom cooked supper. I snuck into my room and shoved a change of clothes into a croaker sack (a burlap bag used to hold feed for livestock). I carefully pocketed all of the money I had—just seventy-five cents. Then, with an empty stomach and only one thought in my head—to get out *fast*—I reached for my sack, ready to head out the door.

Just then, my mom called out, "Ardist, go fill the box with stove wood!"

I went into the kitchen, grabbed the box that we used to fuel the stove, ran outside, and filled it faster than I'd ever done before. Then I grabbed my little sack and ran out the door, quick like a fox.

I ran past the hog pin and up to the barn. Picking up my stashed jacket, I looked back long enough to make sure no one saw me. For a second, I let myself realize that I was going for good. I could see the dark outline of our little house and all of the activity inside it.

I didn't think about how they'd react when I didn't come to the supper table. I didn't think about how much I'd miss my family. I didn't think about where I would go, how I was going to eat, or how I'd take care of myself. I was so overwhelmed with the desire to run that I didn't think at all. I just turned and ran towards my new life, wherever and whatever it was.

Looking back, my running away felt predestined as if I didn't have any choice, but it was out of character to separate myself from my family. As far back as I can remember, I was always the one who loved having my family next to me. When Micah left for the war, it hurt me very badly, and I cried and cried because our family wasn't together anymore. When he came home a time or two on furlough, the whole family followed him down to the train station in the nearby town of Delhi to see him off, and I cried because I hated to see him leave. I surprised the family—and myself—by leaving. I was probably the last person they expected to do that.

I never said goodbye. The last words my mom said to me were to fill the stove wood box. I knew when she found out I ran away, she would be deeply hurt. Years later, when I returned as a grown man, she never questioned why I left. Even though she never said anything, I knew her heart and the love she had for her children, and it was clear that I hurt her that night. However, my only comfort is her knowing how my sudden departure was necessary to help the family. By leaving, I changed the lives of my brothers and sisters forever. I was like Moses, taking his people from a hard life under Pharaoh's grip and leading them into the Promised Land. Exodus 3:7 says, "The Lord said, 'I have surely seen the affliction of My people who are in Egypt.'" Exodus 4:12 says, "Now therefore go, and I will be with thy mouth, and teach thee what thou shalt say."

Thinking back now, I realize that the pressure of being chief plowboy wasn't the only reason for leaving. I also wanted a better life for myself away from the South. The way the white folks treated us, even at my young age, I knew I deserved better and wanted to live it.

Uncle Michael's House

Full of adrenaline and overtaken by the strong desire to leave as quickly as possible, I ran all the way up to the trail leading to town. My mother's brother, Uncle Michael, lived about two miles away. I could have slowed down once I reached the trail because the trees kept me safely hidden, but I didn't dare. I didn't know this uncle very well, and I could have easily run to plenty of other relatives that night, so why I chose him, I don't know. I just let my instinctive feeling take me where it wanted to go.

I ran so fast that I reached him in less than 15 minutes. He and his wife, Midge, were sitting on the porch as most folks did in the evening. I stopped a few feet from the porch, not knowing if I was welcome and knowing how strange it must look to show up so late in the evening. Uncle Michael looked at me, full of surprise.'

"Hello, boy! What are you doin' over here? Do your mom and dad know where you are?"

I felt a long, long way from home.

"Boy, what are you doin' here?"

I stood in front of Uncle Michael's porch, feeling so anxious that I couldn't speak. At that moment, the weight of what I had just done hit me.

In a nervous voice, I replied, "No, sir. I run away."

"Boy, your dad goin' to tan your hide!" I must have looked scared because he changed his tone slightly. "Come, take a seat and tell me what's wrong. Where you goin' to stay?"

I pulled up all of my courage, confessing, "I want to stay with you."

Uncle Michael didn't answer. While he took his time thinking over the situation, my nervousness worsened and I started to panic. If he rejected me, I didn't know where I'd run next.

After two or three minutes, I eagerly offered, "I can work. I know how to do just 'bout anything that's done on a farm."

He calmly answered, "We'll see."

I didn't know what that meant.

We continued sitting on the porch for the next hour, reminiscing about various family members. As was the custom back then, a ball of rags burned nearby so the smoke could keep mosquitoes away. When the smoke began dying out, Aunt Midge noticed the mosquitoes attacking us. She called out my name, suggesting we go inside, which was the first sign that I was welcome. Boy, was I relieved!

Inside, my aunt offered me tea and a piece of cake. After all the excitement and missing supper, I gladly accepted. Soon after, she showed me where to fix my place to sleep. I felt so grateful that I could've slept on the porch with the mosquitoes, under a tree, on the kitchen floor ... anywhere.

The next morning, I rose before the adults, walked out onto the porch and looked around. I let the thoughts sink in that this was my first day out of my dad's house. I realized that I was a man now, on my own, and I needed to make a living. I didn't feel happy or sad, just mixed up inside and excited. The only thing I was sure of was a deep yearning and desire to find whatever was calling me.

Not long afterwards, I heard Aunt Midge get up and pour water into a wash pan. She fixed one of those big, country breakfasts with heaps of bacon, potatoes, fresh biscuits, and eggs. Uncle Michael called me to eat.

As we sat at the table, I offered a verse during the prayer, and then dug into breakfast hungrier than I'd been in a long time. After we finished, my uncle started his work outside. I stayed inside doing whatever my aunt asked of me, which wasn't much. She asked me to pump the water, but priming their pump wasn't easy and required some skill. You had to hold your hand over the opening in order to create suction, and move the handle up and down until you finally drew water up from the ground.

It was Thursday—a school day—but I already decided that I was done with school. I didn't want anyone knowing where I was and I didn't like school anyway, so there didn't seem any reason to go back. With nothing to do, I played most of the day more to occupy my time than to have fun.

By the second night, my uncle still hadn't given me pressure about my plans, and my aunt never asked, "Ardist, don't you think it's time for you to go back to your dad?"

Since my uncle and I didn't say anything, I heard what I wanted to hear.

I heard myself quietly saying, "I found me a new home."

I didn't let myself think too much for fear of what I'd realize. I appreciated how kind my aunt and uncle were to welcome me into their home, and that's all I allowed myself to think. By Saturday, neither my aunt nor uncle hinted at my leaving, so I felt secure that I was there for good.

Saturdays in Delhi

On Saturdays, there wasn't much for most of the grown folks to do, so they often walked to the nearby town of Delhi—a place to have fun, let loose, and let the good times roll. Many country people shopped at Delhi for clothes and food. One of the main attractions was a little place where coloreds could drink and dance. Even those who didn't drink or dance visited Delhi every Saturday to stand under a big tree and talk, or stand around visiting in one of the two cafeterias run by coloreds.

For most men, gathering in Delhi every Saturday was a major social event because the men spent their time catching up with friends and family while the women stayed at home. My dad looked forward to standing for hours, crowded underneath a big old tree, talking with his friends.

I was so used to men going to Delhi every Saturday that I didn't think much of it when Uncle Michael walked there one afternoon. However, when he returned that evening, my world changed. He walked up to the house where I sat on the porch swing, enjoying the cool evening air and sat down next to me.

"How you doin', boy?"

"Just fine, sir."

"I saw your dad today. He said he have a house on the Warden Lane and he don't see why you staying over here with me."

Hearing that, my heart pumped faster than the wings of a hummingbird. My blood pressure must have jumped from normal to the highest you could go without having a stroke. Even at my young age, I understood enough to know how grownups respected each other.

Although unspoken, my uncle's words clearly told me, "Ardist, you can't stay with me any longer. Your dad has spoken."

I also understood that I couldn't go back home because, in training his children, my dad always made it clear that, "If you can't abide by the rules of my house, there's the door."

My dad didn't say much to Uncle Michael, but his few words conveyed a lot. He also implied that if I really were the prodigal son, journeying to a far place to make something of myself, then I shouldn't hang around like a broken limb on a tree, and shame on me if I did. My dad didn't tell me directly or express it in so many words, but his message was clear.

I started thinking about how my life always involved the support of my family. My father provided a roof over my head, and food on the table three meals a day, seven days a week. He gave me a place to lie down at night, a change of clothes, and two pairs of shoes. Love from Mom, my sisters, and my brothers filled me up. I left all of that comfort and surety to become a vagabond—homeless and alone.

Before I felt too sorry for myself, I realized that I always had family support. I wasn't alone. Family will see me through my journey—wherever the journey took me.

Time to Move On

Knowing I had to leave Uncle Michael and Aunt Midge's house, I got the unction to journey to Aunt Margaret's home, which was 10 miles away in Oak Grove. Once again, no goodbye, no discussions with anyone, no preplanning, and no forewarning to let my aunt know I was coming.

All I knew for sure was that my guardian angel would show me where to go next, and my angel was guiding me to Aunt Margaret. Why her? I don't know that any more than why I ran to Uncle Michael's a few nights earlier. Like Uncle Michael, Aunt Margaret hardly knew me.

The next morning before sunup, I ran out of the house before the grownups rose. I had nothing to face the world with except the seventy-five cents in my pocket and a wrinkled change of clothes stuffed inside an old feed sack. Surprisingly, I didn't feel scared or insecure. I didn't feel worried. I didn't even pause long enough to figure out how to get to Oak Grove.

Once again, I let the driving force that pulled me out of my family home pull me to Oak Grove. Up to that point, the furthest I'd ever been from home was Delhi, which was about three miles from the farm, and always with the company of my family. Somehow, I knew what to do that morning.

I walked to Delhi, found a Greyhound bus, paid the fifty cent fare, and walked to the back of the bus where coloreds sat. At that time, white people allowed coloreds two seats on the bus. If it was crowded, we had to stand; if it was too crowded to stand, we had to get off and wait for the next bus.

As the bus stopped along the way, picking up people and dropping them off, I feared that someone would recognize me.

Throughout the community, my father was well known; everyone who knew my father knew all of his children. Amazingly, I made it all the way to Oak Grove without running into anyone. My guardian angel was watching over me.

Oak Grove's New Arrival

Oak Grove was a small town, but we looked at our relatives there as city folks because they weren't farmers. Oak Grove was less friendly towards coloreds than Warden was—another mystery to the puzzle of why I chose to go there.

I arrived late in the afternoon not knowing where Aunt Margaret lived, but, if I asked around, I knew I'd find her. In those days, all the colored folks in a community knew each other. I walked up to someone at the bus station, gave my aunt's name and explained that I was her nephew.

One of the women said, "Get on that trail alongside the railroad track and follow it about a mile. You'll see two shotgun houses on the left side of the railroad. The one in the back is your Aunt Margaret. The one in front is Alyssa. You know her?"

"Yes, ma'am," I responded, "I know her. She's my cousin and the principal of the colored school."

I thanked the woman and walked down the road. I was still on autopilot, not feeling nervous or thinking much of anything. I just knew that it was where I was supposed to go for now.

When I arrived, Aunt Margaret was visiting with my cousin Alyssa. In traditional southern style, they were sitting on Alyssa's porch talking. They recognized me immediately and welcomed me with a loud greeting.

"Hello, boy! You a long way from home! What in the world are you doin' up here? Is somethin' wrong?"

As I stood facing them, I suddenly felt all of the fear that was mysteriously missing during my journey up there and my voice shook as I answered.

"The only thing wrong is I have run away from home. I stayed with Uncle Michael and and Aunt Midge for the past few days.

Then my dad found out about it. I guess Uncle Michael told him in Delhi on Saturday, and Dad said he don't see why I am stayin' there with him since he have a house on the Warden Lane. I knew what that meant. I ran away from there to here. Uncle don't know where I am and I'm afraid to go back home."

Aunt Margaret listened to the whole story, and then asked, "Well, what do you wanna do?"

"I wanna stay here."

Aunt Margaret and Cousin Alyssa discussed it for a few minutes because they weren't sure if it was a good idea. I sat there, watching them talk on the porch in low voices. It seemed like an hour went by without them coming to an answer.

I started to worry, asking myself, "Oh, what have I done?"

Just then, my guardian angel made a way for me again.

Aunt Margaret said that I could stay with her. *Hallelujah!* Cousin Alyssa said I was late to start the school year, but if I wanted to stay with Aunt Margaret, I had to enroll in school right away. Although I still hated school, I eagerly submitted to any condition they set in front of me.

I settled into the second shelter of my journey. Aunt Margaret had a nice house. Even after living with her, I never knew exactly what she did. I just knew that she worked in town and wasn't a farmer.

The next day, I registered for class at Seat Grove High. I was 12 years old and in the fourth grade. The school was much larger than the little country school back in Warden. It was exciting to see all of the children and teachers. Their basketball field, located outside in the dirt like all of the other colored schools, was larger than Warden's field. Seat Grove High had another large area where you could play softball since baseball wasn't yet popular in schools. The children were friendly and asked many questions, as children do.

"Where you from?"

"How long you goin' to stay?"

"Do you have any brothers and sisters?"

"Who do you live with?"

"Where's your mom and dad?"

Children know how to ask all of the questions you don't want to talk about. I was so shy and closed mouthed that it took a very long time before I knew most of the children in my class. Of course, when I did say anything, I made up most of the answers, telling them what I wanted them to hear.

Chapter 7

Mr. Johnson

Fears and Insecurities

Our fourth grade teacher, Mr. Johnson, was serious when it came to our learning. On my first day, he kept me in during recess. Cousin Alyssa told him I was her cousin and he made it clear that he didn't play favorites. I needed to do extra catch-up studying because I started so late. I adjusted to the class reasonably well and was an average participator. Just like back home, I struggled every time I stood in front of the class reading aloud.

Mr. Johnson had a unique way of giving our spelling test. In class, we all sat in rows; then, depending on the day, Mr. Johnson picked a certain row to stand in front of the class. He divided the girls in one row and had the boys face them—boys against girls. Just like back home, the girls were usually better spellers, so they often won. I was never a good speller before, but standing with the other children encouraged me to study. I felt more confident and became a better student by controlling my emotions and focusing on learning rather than fearing what I thought I couldn't do.

The insecurities, which drove me from home, were still with me. No matter how hard I tried, I couldn't pass my classes. I believed that I was doing my best but, somewhere deep inside, fear kept me from doing my best. I was scared that I couldn't measure up. I was scared of what people would think if they knew that I ran away from home. I was scared that I'd disappoint the adults I tried to please and they'd think I wasn't trying. I was scared of shaming my Aunt Margaret and Cousin Alyssa. I was scared that they'd regret letting me stay with them and send me home.

Mr. Johnson may have noticed the unspoken fears swirling in my head. He gave me a little relief, saying that most adults can tell if a child is serious or playing around in doing their lesson. I felt that he must have known how hard I was trying, even though I wasn't meeting normal standards.

The Lure of the City

One of my favorite times in class was when Mr. Johnson told stories about his world experiences. At one point, he left Louisiana's Oak Grove to work in Oakland and San Francisco in California. Like thousands of other colored people discovered, working in the city wasn't what he expected and, a few months later, he returned to Oak Grove.

That experience helped him realize something that he tried to teach us. He explained how people's mindset changed rapidly since the war started. It was true that colored folks had more op-portunities in the cities, thinking the good times were finally here, and they lived like there was no tomorrow; however, the massive social changes didn't happen the way they expected.Disappointed, many coloreds said, "Tomorrow will never come." Mr. Johnson said that was an untrue statement. The Bible tells us in Second Kings 7:1, *"Elisha prophesieth hear ye the word of the Lord: Thus saith the Lord, Tomorrow about this time something special would happen."*

Mr. Johnson brought in postcards from San Francisco, show-ing us tall buildings like nothing we had ever seen. It was the first time I saw a picture of San Francisco. The city looked so beauti-ful. I never dreamed that I'd get out of the South and go there. I enjoyed Mr. Johnson's stories as he gave us real-life information about what another part of America offered. The class was always on the edge of their seats listening.

Like other children, I heard about big cities like San Francisco and Chicago from people who went there and then returned for funerals or visits. They came back wearing fancier clothes, talking about doing certain things, and showing off how well they were doing in their new world. The way they talked about California, it sounded like heaven on earth. Unlike Mr. Johnson, they left out the fine print, never telling the truth of how whites still treated them as second-class citizens. The wildness and glamour of city life didn't impress him, and he told us that California wasn't all that they said it was.

Mr. Johnson observed that whites treated coloreds a little better in California because colored didn't have to say, "Yes, sir" and "No, ma'am," which was a big thing to us back then. It was even enough to make us want to go there. He said that coloreds made more money in the city, but that was mostly because everything was so much more expensive there. He told us not to believe that everything was so different in the cities. Coloreds were still controlled, could only live in certain areas with other coloreds, and go to colored-only nightclubs. Mr. Johnson made sure we understood that, in the city, whites and colored mixed, but being "colored" followed you wherever you went.

"You have to work hard, and you got to know somethin' to get a job out there."

When coloreds came back to Louisiana for visits, talking about how they had better jobs, it was only because they were making so much more than they made back home. Even so, they still worked secondary jobs because the white man got the administrative, management, and other good-time jobs. Coloreds were still taking orders from the white man, just on a higher plane.

"You guys better *learn* something," Mr. Johnson warned. "Learn how to read and write and be leaders!"

That all sounded good, but I didn't know what he was talking about. I couldn't understand the idea of leadership and especially never thought of supervising anyone. Like most colored folks in those days, I only knew what they taught me; that is, I knew how to follow. Most of the coloreds back then weren't thinking about going to California to become leaders. They were only thinking of getting a better job and making more money.

Hearing Mr. Johnson's stories and looking at all of those post-cards, I decided that, if I ever left Oak Grove, I wanted to live in Chicago. I remembered that I had a cousin somewhere in Chicago and planned to make a living there. I couldn't even guess what I would do since all I knew was farming. My cousin hadn't been back to Louisiana for a visit and I didn't know him that well; however, if I found him, I thought that he would take me in. All I needed to do was get there. I figured that, if I always lived with family, I'd make it through my journey, wherever it took me.

Test Time

It was getting late in the school year. Test time was coming soon and I was terribly anxious. No matter how hard I tried, I couldn't remember all of the things I was taught. Even with help from Aunt Margaret, Cousin Alyssa, and the other children, I was only getting Cs and Ds in class. I got a B in math, but that wasn't enough to pass the fourth grade. After taking the end-of-year tests, I waited anxiously for the report card. When it came, it said that I didn't pass fourth grade. I couldn't retake the tests, so I had to repeat the fourth grade.

I went into spasms and hysteria, panicking about my aunt and cousin's reaction over my report card. I hid it for two days before I pulled together enough courage to tell them about my failure. Of course, all that time I hid my report card, they already knew—Cousin Alyssa was the principal!

They had already decided that I was going to repeat fourth grade. Knowing that made the strong pull come back, telling me that it was time to move on again. I couldn't face going back to Mr. Johnson's fourth-grade class. The other children would laugh and tease me, and wouldn't stop no matter how badly it hurt. I could hear them laughing at me.

"You big dummy! You couldn't even pass the fourth grade!"

I just couldn't face it.

Making Money

Summer break came, but Aunt Margaret did not allow me to be idle. While I waited for school to start up again, she told me that people needed their grass cut, and I could make a nice little bit of money by charging thirty-five to fifty cents a yard. I tried to look happy, but inside I was restless, trying to figure out my escape.

I did everything I could to make as much money as possible. In addition to cutting grass, I ran to the store for older people, who paid me ten cents a run, and Aunt Margaret's friends gave me odd jobs now and again. Aunt Margaret was a good-looking girl, and one of her male friends, Tom, really liked her. He probably thought that, if he kept paying me to do odd jobs, it would attract her attention. He had a small farm and, since I knew that work well, I did everything he asked with the efficiency my dad taught us.

Tom paid me fifty cents for some jobs and sometimes a few dollars for others. He always paid something because he liked how I worked.

"Now, when farming time comes, you work with me," he said. "I'll even give you a whole bale of cotton!"

I was interested in that idea because a bale fetched around $40 or $50 back then. However, as excited as I was about having so much money, it meant that I had to stay through the school year. I just couldn't bear that, so I kept working odd jobs and saving most of the money. Within two months, I saved $32.

The Movies and the Telegram Post

I always loved watching movies at the theater. During the summer, I treated myself to one movie every weekend, which cost fifteen cents. One time, I went to see the early showing of a movie about Jackie Robinson. All of the advertisements said the picture was uplifting, performed with great visuals, and spoken with eloquence. I worked all week, and was so excited about seeing Jackie Robinson that I could hardly wait for the weekend to come.

Back then, coloreds sat upstairs in the movie house balcony and whites did not allow them to use the bathrooms. Towards the end of the movie, I had to relieve myself but didn't want to miss any part of the movie. I held on until the end but was ready to burst by then. I ran outside and had to go so badly, I knew I couldn't make it all the way home.

Looking around, I saw a telegram post between the movie theater and the gas station next to it. It seemed like a secluded enough place for me to relieve myself without someone seeing me. Less than five seconds into it, the town sheriff and his deputy drove up, flashing their red lights.

The deputy shouted, "Nigger, *get in the car!*"

Scared out of my skin, I made haste, climbing into the sheriff's car.

"What do you think you're doing?"

Before I could answer, the deputy turned to the sheriff.

"Let's beat this nigger. Suppose a white woman would've come by and seen him?"

He then turned back to me, yelling, and almost begged the sheriff for permission to beat me. I was already scared of white men, but imagine how scared I was, sitting there with two of them who were carrying guns, calling me nigger, and threatening to beat me! I thought for sure that this was the end of my short life.

It went on for a while, with the deputy yelling at me and then telling the sheriff they should beat me. I was so scared at that point that I couldn't speak or move. The sheriff had a reputation for hating coloreds and had no hesitation about killing us, young or old. However, each time the deputy begged, the sheriff said that they were not going to beat me no matter how excited the deputy became.

Right when I thought my life was over, the sheriff asked, "Boy, you got any money?"

I was shaking so hard that I could barely answer, "Yes, sir. I have $10."

"Give it to me and get out of town! Don't let me see you in this area again."

I gave him the money and, as soon as the car door opened, I moved like a fox with hounds chasing it.

That experience scared me so much that I don't like thinking about it, even now. I thank my guardian angel for protecting me in that car. My testimony shall ever be that the Lord spared me that very day.

I ran straight to Aunt Margaret's house, too scared to tell her what happened. More than ever, I knew I needed to leave Oak Grove soon, but I didn't know where to go. Within days, my guardian angel showed me the way again when I stumbled upon a letter addressed to Aunt Margaret from Uncle Ernest in Oakland, California. I memorized the address on 10th Street and knew that this was my next move.

Off to California

As soon as the house was empty, I left Oak Grove—once again without a plan and without telling anyone goodbye or thank you. I grabbed my few belongings and headed back to Delhi—this time taking the train west. At the train station, I bought a one-way ticket to Oakland for about $25. The train from Delhi to Oakland ran once a day; I didn't know what time of day that was, but my guardian angel made sure I got there just in time.

All of the colored passengers had to sit in the front of the train. I never rode a train before and didn't understand why we had to sit in the back of a bus but sit in front of the train. Before long, I learned why. It was so hot that we had to keep the windows down for air, which let in the soot and other rubbish from the coal and steam engines located right in front of us.

Seeing that I looked so young and was travelling all alone, many adult passengers were concerned. They never badgered me, but they did notice that I looked too young to be all alone, so they took care of me and asked me questions.

"Who you traveling with?"

"Are you hungry?"

"Do you have any changing clothes?"

Because of the grime and grease blowing inside the train, it was customary for passengers to carry a change of clothing so they looked clean and respectable when they arrived at their destination. I didn't know this and only had the shirt I wore. After two days on the train, I arrived in Oakland with my white shirt looking blacker than I was!

During the train ride, I enjoyed all of the attention, becoming talkative and making up stories that I figured the adults wanted to hear. The conversations made the long trip a little more relaxing. When we changed trains halfway through the trip, and crossed the Mason-Dixon Line, the seating restrictions became more open.

When we were just a few hours from Oakland, a number of people who lived there gave me their address. They were honestly concerned about this little country boy all alone in the big city. They asked me to come by and say hello after I settled in with Uncle Ernest.

Now that I was getting closer to Oakland, that doubting voice started up again inside my head.

"How well do I know him? He knows I'm his sister's child, but what if he rejects me? What if I can't find him? Where would I go then? Where would I work?"

I didn't have answers to any of these questions rolling through my head but, for some reason, I still didn't panic. Even after Mr. Johnson's exciting stories, Oakland never impressed me. I didn't feel compelled to live there, but my guardian angel was guiding me, whether I liked it or not. I tried to stop the self-doubt, telling myself that this was where I was destined to go.

In my heart, I knew that I couldn't have made all of the connections to Oakland by myself, so I started to calm down, accepting my destiny. My confidence rose a little by reminding myself how my guardian angel had taken care of me so far and kept me focused. I knew if I kept listening, I'd be fine—even though I didn't know what I'd do once I arrived at my uncle's doorstep.

Chapter 8

My Third Home

Uncle Ernest's Welcome

The 13-year-old vagabond was swiftly arriving at his third home: Oakland, California. I appreciated the graceful kindness awarded me by the other passengers and this kindness continued after I stood at the train depot, unsure of what to do next. Before I knew it, I was safely in a cab. Those good people directed the driver straight to 10th Street and paid my fare. My guardian angel again guided me safely through my impulsive journey.

During the cab ride, I stared out of the window at the strange world. I couldn't believe how tall the buildings were and how closely they all stood next to each other. I missed the open spaces of the farms back home where you have room to run and breathe, and where you can see for miles without having anything get in your way.

I stared out of the cab window, wondering, "What is this new world?"

I passed what seemed like thousands of busy-looking people, all moving swiftly with purpose but seemed to be doing nothing. They weren't fixing anything. They weren't selling, delivering, making, preparing, or cleaning anything, but they sure were in a hurry!

Finally, the cab arrived at 10th Street and Uncle Ernest's rooming house. His wife had left him years ago, returning to her folks in Louisiana; since then, he lived alone. He had a large room, and shared the floor and a common kitchen with three other renters.

When Uncle Ernest saw me, he didn't recognize my face, but he recognized my name. By now, many of my relatives heard that I ran away from home. Like the others, he was surprised to see me at his doorstep but welcomed me inside.

"Boy, do your folks know where you are? I thought you returned home."

"No, sir. Uncle Michael, the first placed I stayed, don't know. Aunt Margaret and Cousin Alyssa in Oak Grove, the second place I stayed, don't know. Each of these families was good to me."

"Then why you movin' from place to place?"

I couldn't explain. I just felt that I had to leave, and keep going wherever I was supposed to go.

Uncle Ernest was a man of few words. He didn't seem vexed with his vagabond nephew, traveling the country on his own, but I could tell he was concerned about my odd actions, so I stuck to the facts.

"I left my dad's house because I was lookin' for a better place. I left Uncle Michael's for fear that he'd send me back to my dad's house. Then I left Aunt Margaret's because I didn't want to face other kids teasing me for repeatin' the fourth grade."

"What are you gonna do here?" he asked. "You too young to do public work. It's not like farmin' where you work as soon as you're big enough."

With great eagerness, I answered, "If I can stay here with you, Uncle, I will find a job. I don't know anything about the city, but I know how to work."

"I don't know. There aren't many jobs for non service people because the military is releasing thousands of veterans. They're comin' back from the wars with Germany and Japan and get the first chance for jobs."

I started to worry that he'd send me home.

"I'll talk with you tomorrow," he continued. "You must be tired. Go in there and clean up. You look like a mess."

It was such a relief to hear him welcome me in. And boy, I *was* a mess! My shirt was so filthy that we threw it away. After that train ride, I swear it took another five years before I'd wear a white shirt again.

I bedded down for the night in my uncle's room without thinking about what I'd do next. For all of my insecurities, I always knew I was a good worker and a fast learner. My dad taught me how to learn by carefully watching others. With that knowledge, I fell asleep knowing that I'd be fine.

Paper Routes and Butcher Shops

The next day, Uncle Ernest instructed me how to conduct myself while he was at work. He introduced me to some of the tenants in the rooming house but never said anything about school. A few days later, I met some children my age who lived on the block. As usual, I was closed mouthed, not wanting to talk about my past and too shy to say much else.

One of the boys had a paper route and let me walk with him to learn the job. He showed me how to fold the papers and explained that I had to make sure I got the paper to the right address.

He also knew three girls who lived across the street from me and, when he came by my building, the girls sat outside and talked with him. If I was outside with him, the girls talked to me, too. After a while, when I sat outside alone, the girls came out to talk but I was so shy. I never knew what to say. I just mostly listened while they talked. I was happy to sit with them and the interaction relieved some of the loneliness from missing my family.

Three days after I showed up at Uncle Ernest's house, he sat me down and asked how I liked Oakland so far. I said it was fine, but he could sense the loneliness in my expression.

"I notified your mom and dad that you are here in Oakland. Are you ready to return home?"

Suddenly, my journey snapped into focus. For the first time, I clearly understood why my guardian angel guided me out of Warden.

"Oh, no, Uncle! I am going to make a lot of money and get my family out here!"

He didn't say anything, but I could tell he still wanted to send me back home, no matter how selfless my goal.

Knowing in my heart what I must do, I remained determined to succeed, so I doubled my efforts to find a job. Four days later, the family who lived on the ground floor of the rooming house helped me get a part-time job cleaning a little mom-and-pop butcher shop on the corner. I was so happy to work that I said yes without asking about the pay.

When I heard that they would pay me $3 to go in once a week, I couldn't believe it. Three whole dollars! I never imagined I'd make so much in just one day. For the first time since running from home, joy filled my soul. Being used to farm work, cleaning the butcher shop was easy. It only took me two hours to mop the floor, scrub the counters, put everything away, and clean the meat-cutting machines. I was very thorough and the place sparkled. A white-glove inspection wouldn't find any grease or dirt.

The girls across the street and the paperboy often talked about the cowboy movies playing at the Rex and Broadway theaters. I hadn't seen a movie since that frightening incident in Oak Grove, and I never dared ask my uncle for money. So, when my first pay-day came, I decided that I would treat myself to a movie. At that time, one show cost thirty-five cents and you could see the second show for another nickel. I made it my little tradition every payday to spend forty cents at either the Rex or Broadway movie houses. I loved movies so much that I sat in the movie house, watching the same movie over and over again until they kicked me out. My weekly movies were the only luxury I allowed myself. I remained focused on sending money home each week, hoping to bring my family out west.

Canning Season

A few months later, canning season started. The family who set me up with the butcher shop job told my uncle that, if I wanted more work, their employer, the Delaminate Cannery in Oakland, was hiring for the season. When Uncle Ernest took me down to apply, the hiring manager looked at me, no doubt thinking I looked too young.

It was 1945 and I looked all of 13 and nothing more. Actually, I'm not even sure if I had a social security number. However, my guardian angel blessed me again, for the manager never asked my age and hired me on the spot.

I couldn't believe my fortune! Now I had a second job making $1.08 an hour, which was more than most people back home made in an entire day of hard labor. I started work immediately, standing in an area of the conveyor belt and carrying empty cans to the fruit-filling machine. My job was to make sure the cans moved along smoothly without backing up. I mastered that job quickly and kept the job for the whole season.

When my shift ended, I continued working the swing shift, cleaning the plant for the morning shift. As a country boy, there isn't such a thing as night work since we worked by the sun. Unfamiliar to such hours, I would sometimes fall asleep on the bus ride home and pass my stop. I'd get off the bus, lost in some unfamiliar neighborhood, and ask around for directions and walk back home. While working double shifts at the cannery, I kept my job at the butcher shop, too.

Once in a while, I wrote a short letter home, explaining my new life. People back home had a hard time believing that, if I worked past my eight-hour shift, the boss considered it overtime and paid me extra per hour. I think everyone except Mom (and maybe Dad) thought I was lying about the overtime until I received my first paycheck from the cannery and sent most of it home.

When I first saw the numbers typed on my check, I shouted with joy. I was going to free my family for sure and bring them out to California for a better life. I imagined that my shout was like the victorious Battle of Jericho. When the Israelites shouted so loudly, they collapsed the walls. Joshua 6:5 says, "And it shall come to pass, that when they make a long blast with the ram's horn, and when ye hear the sound of the trumpet, all the people shall shout with a great shout."

I sent most of my checks home to Mom, but I knew Dad got them because he ruled the household under poisonous pedagogy. I continued these double shifts until canning season ended three months later.

Trying Tomatoes

Although my high-paying job at the cannery ended, I had no stress because I had faith that I would always find a job. I learned about going down to the unemployment office to apply for work. While there, I listened to a few workers tell me to pick tomatoes. It cost $2 a day to catch the truck that drove you down to the fields. That was a lot of money, but many of these tomato pickers were so good that they could make $10 to $15 a day.

Even with my extensive farming background, I was terrible at picking tomatoes. Without any previous practice, I didn't know how to pick the right size at the right stage of ripeness. When I took in my tomatoes for weighing, the paymaster graded my tomatoes. He sorted the good ones into a credit basket and the bad ones in a debit basket. After a whole day of bending near to the ground picking tomatoes, I didn't make enough to cover my ride to the field. The high-paying and easier work from the cannery spoiled me. After one day picking tomatoes, I never returned.

Life on the Railroad

The next day, I sat at the unemployment office, hoping for something other than tomato picking. While waiting my turn in line, I noticed a signup sheet taped to the wall that said, "Southern Pacific Railroad needs extra gang workers. Report to the S.P. boarding house tomorrow for assignment."

The railroad sounded so secure, and I pictured myself working there until retirement. I didn't know what an extra gang worker was, but it was work and I felt confident that I could learn any type of work, so I signed up. All they asked was my name and address; I prayed they wouldn't ask my age.

The following day, I reported to the Southern Pacific bunkhouse for orientation. The other men were between the ages of 19 to early thirties. Compared to these grown men, I looked young. Many of them looked at me and some said aloud what they all were probably thinking.

"Boy, you look awfully *young* to be here."

I never answered. I just stood quietly, trying to look like an adult. No one ever asked my age directly but just kept saying that I looked young. When my turn came up for review, the foreman looked at me long and hard.

"How old are you?"

I stared straight at him.

"Nineteen, sir."

I don't know if he knew I was lying and he never asked for proof.

I joined 10 other new workers. We earned $1.35 an hour, but we didn't get it all. As railroad employees, we ate and slept at the boarding house, and they took our rent out of our paychecks before we saw it. Without our own kitchen, Southern Pacific provided three square meals a day, whether you ate them or not, which were taken out of your pay too.

We ate breakfast before leaving for work and then returned for lunch. If we worked too far from the boarding house, the foreman decided whether they should deliver dinner. Either way, you always ate dinner at the same time. The boarding house served supper between certain hours; if you got there too late, you didn't eat but they still charged you. Weekends had a different schedule, and they still charged you for all three meals.

Our payday was on the first and fifteenth of every month, and we could transfer to a section gang after six months. After six months, you could earn credits towards free travel wherever Southern Pacific trains went. We were assigned two foremen, and

Alvin, the one assigned to us, determined where we bunked. After we signed in for our new jobs, they told us to go home and gather what we needed for work: clothing, work boots, gloves, and a few personal effects. Then they told us to come back the same night to settle in because work would begin early the next morning.

All of this news excited me. Making $1.35 an hour was the highest I made up to that point. I felt rich! I also felt like an adult, having my own space and three meals a day, which I paid for myself. Yes, I was becoming a man. My only worry was leaving Uncle Ernest.

As excited as I was to start my new life, I had always been with family up to that point. That night, I talked to Uncle Ernest, explaining my new job. He didn't say much as I gathered my few things. He only agreed that I should leave my church clothes with him.

I returned to the boarding house, acting as grown up as I could while I settled into my bunk and chatted with the other men.

One or two asked, "You're kinda young for this type of work, aren't you?"

Not knowing what type of work it was, I honestly told them I didn't think so.

The next morning, I quickly learned what they meant by being "too young." As hard as we all worked back on the farm, thinking it was the toughest labor imaginable, it was nothing compared to being an extra gang worker. They do all of the tough and rugged jobs that regular section gang workers don't want to do. It's the hardest of the hard and the lowest of the low.

The first two weeks were an extremely trying time for me. On my first day, they put me on the air compressor, which is like a giant jackhammer run by air. The air compressor was so heavy that I could barely drag it more than a few feet at a time. Then, it tossed my skinny body around so badly that I kept shaking hours later when I was in bed.

It took me nearly six weeks to learn the skills of an extra gang worker, which was to maintain the tracks. No machinery existed for this task; it was strictly manual labor. I helped replace miles of 20-foot iron tracks. We replaced worn crossties and used a pry bar-looking tool to pack ¾- to 2-inch rocks under the crossties. Then we removed old concrete with an air-gun tool, which looked similar to a jackhammer.

After a few weeks, I learned how to swing the hammer well enough to spike the rails down to the crossties. Although the other men looked out for me, they treated me as if I were full grown and expected me to do my share. I did everything I could not to let them down.

The high railroad pay was misleading because half of your pay went to room and food before you saw your paycheck. Even though they provided you three squares a day, you needed to eat that well to maintain the strenuous physical demands of your job. If someone asked me if they should choose between farming and being an extra gang worker, I'd say that farming—with all the cheating, suppression, and racism of the South—was still a much better life.

My foreman, Alvin, impressed me. He was Spanish, knew his job well, and was very good at handling the spiking hammer. Besides me, the crew had one seasoned colored worker named Milton, and the rest of the extra gang workers were mostly Spanish. Alvin wasn't just there to order us around. Sometimes he laid long stretches of track, spiking for hours. He and Milton took turns on the hammer. They moved very fast, and we had to stay ahead of them, laying track and tamping down the crossties.

In contrast to society around us, we never had a problem working together—white, Spanish, and colored all in one crew. Everyone carried his fair share of the work. I was about 14 years old then and carried my share like all of the adults.

Those were good days when men worked hard. Then after work, they dressed up in nice clothes and went out for a good time. Sometimes, they took me; when that happened, I tried to fit in by drinking beer. I never tried alcohol before and soon found that two sips was my limit. Hanging with the men in those noisy, smoked-filled bars wasn't as enjoyable as I thought it would be. I always preferred the peaceful, clean air of the country at night, sitting on the porch, listening to the crickets and frogs talking.

Sometimes the men had such a good time going heavy on the liquor that they showed up for work the next morning singing the popular phrase, "I sure had a wonderful time last night ... that is, my sidekicks say I did!"

What I liked best about going out with the men was listening to the down-home blues played at some of the bars. However, even that wasn't always joyous because, once in a while, a song came up that was so sad, it made me wonder why I ever left home. All through my railroad days, I questioned my rash running from the farm. Hearing those sad blues just pulled out all of my doubt, homesickness, and sadness that I tried to hide from others and from myself. No matter how you try to ignore something by stuffing it in the back of your mind, it always has a way of coming out and making you face it.

My job at the railroad was my jump from childhood to full-fledged adulthood. For the first time in my life, I didn't have family to talk to or to help me. I was all alone, bunking with grown men, paying for my own room and board, and making decisions that directly affected my survival.

As with most people in a new environment, I picked up some good habits and some bad. I always had a good work ethic, since my dad's watchful eye wouldn't allow anything less. Somehow, the railroad increased my work ethic and I was proud of how hard I worked each day. On the down side, I picked up the habit of cursing and using words I never thought of or dared use back home. I also picked up a dozen or so different gambling games the men played to pass the time after work.

During all of these opportunities to make good and bad decisions, I stayed focused on my goal to bring my family out of Louisiana. This helped me ignore negative confrontations, not letting anyone incite me to do something I'd regret. By focusing on my goal, I also stayed away from nonprofitable socializing. This helped me continue saving money while other men used it up letting the good times roll.

A few times, I visited Uncle Ernest on the weekends. I told him how much I liked my job and the men I worked with. I told him all the things I thought adults wanted to hear and held back the full story. Early in life, I learned that adults only wanted to hear certain things and it's not worth upsetting them by sharing too much.

Restless Again

In my confused and limited adolescent mind, there were times when I forgot about God and being grateful. Then, moments came when I was in despair or great sadness. At those times, a door or window opened just enough for me to go forward but not enough for me to be lifted up in pride. It was God's reminder that all of my accomplishments so far weren't solely from my own doing. He kept me from losing myself in pride, remembering that God was using me for a greater, useful purpose.

Although this reminder sustained me through the exhaustion and physical pain from working so hard, I felt myself growing restless and weary again. The work was too strenuous and my money stack was growing too slowly. I didn't waste any money, but I never seemed to have much saved at the end of the month. I didn't know how to budget or plan a savings for my family's trip west. I just figured I'd have enough when the money stack seemed big. Then I wondered if I was sending too much money home and not leaving enough for savings.

Either way, I knew that it was time to move on and find a better pasture. Where the pasture lay, I had no idea. It didn't bother me because I now accepted the fact that I never had a plan since leaving my dad's house and never knew my next step. One thing I was very sure of: When the yearning for something new grew inside me, my guardian angel would once again show me the way.

Chapter 9

The Desert

Spill on the Tracks

Months passed and I continued to think about a greener pasture. Christmas was near and a voice inside tried to convince me that I had a good life at the railroads. I had a job, a comfortable place to stay, and three hearty meals a day. Although I'd been there for nearly a year, the extra gang work wasn't coming any easier, but I could handle it. I had to settle down and really ask myself if leaving made any sense. I liked how the men all looked out for each other (mostly, they looked out for me). I wondered if I should rebel against all of this or remain in my comfort zone. My answer came a few weeks later.

Right around the first of the year in 1947, one of the evening freight trains had an accident, spilling some type of oil or chemical all over the tracks. We rushed over there as the cleanup crew, doing the dirty work as extra gang hands did. I remember that time as the coldest night and day in Oakland—maybe because my Louisiana clothes weren't warm enough for the Oakland winters. I did learn that no matter how cold a human body gets, it could keep moving.

The cleanup was long and tedious. Finally, sometime after sun-up, the top brass allowed us to stop and we trucked back to the bunkhouse. They had hot coffee, tea, and sandwiches waiting for us. We ate quickly and went straight to bed. We were so bushed that the railroad gave us the day off—without pay of course. That cleanup experience convinced me that it was time to look for the greener pasture.

Heading for Herlong

I woke up around late morning, got dressed in my good clothes, didn't bother with dinner, and headed straight for the unemployment office. I found army officers in there, soliciting people to work in Herlong, California. I filled out another short application, much like the one for Southern Pacific, eagerly jumping at the possible new job with nearly 50 other men.

Most of them asked, "Where's Herlong?"

Like me, they didn't care so long as they got the job.

I had no thought of resigning from the railroad job. I went to the bunkhouse and got my few personal items. There were no goodbyes. Again, my guardian angel guided me. That act of grace and mercy helped me get a day off at the right time to go to the unemployment office and land a federal civil service job in a town in which I was destined to be for the next eight years.

After filling out the short application, we all stood around the unemployment office waiting for further instructions. An hour passed before the army officer gave each of us directions and a pass on the Western Pacific train going towards Salt Lake City. Herlong was the first stop, eight hours travel from Oakland. Upon our arrival, a required physical examination would secure the job; if anyone failed the exam, the same free train pass would return him to Oakland. The army officer gave us three days to check in for the physical examination.

I was excited about the new job adventure, but then self-doubting thoughts started to overtake my happiness. I wondered what the new job would be like. I didn't know where I'd stay. I started to feel sad that I was leaving Uncle Ernest and moving to an area with no family or anyone I knew for miles. After a while, a consoling thought uplifted my heart again: I remembered that I never had a plan before, it had taken me this far, and it had always worked out for the better.

The next day, a trusted adult reminded me that you had to be at least 18 years old to work for the government, just like the draft. I wasn't quite 15 years old and started to panic. I must have looked like I was going to boil over, and the adult tried to console me.

"Calm down, young fellow! Do you have an older brother back home who's 18?"

"Yes. My brother Caleb's 19 or a bit more."

"Then use his name and date of birth," he suggested easily.

I was silent for a few minutes, thinking about the dishonesty verses losing the job. Finally, I answered.

"Sir, tell me how I may do this."

"Write and ask your mom for his date of birth and his birth certificate."

I started to panic again.

"Writing will take too long. I have to report for check in within three days."

"Do your folks have a telephone?"

"Why, yes, I think they do. They live in Monroe, Louisiana."

"Then ask your uncle if he has the number. If he has it, I will call them for you. Ask your mom for Caleb's date of birth and see if she will send you his birth certificate."

I called Mom. She told me Caleb's date of birth and said that she'd look for his birth certificate. I kept the conversation short, so Mom didn't have a clue what I had in mind. She never questioned me because she thought of me as trustworthy.

I arrived in Herlong early the next morning—January 17, 1947. Looking over the small town, I wasn't sure what to think. You could see the length and width of the entire town from the train depot, and I could hear big sighs from the other new employees.

"Is this it?"

My Life as Caleb

We arrived very early, so we had to mill around waiting for the personnel office to open a couple of hours later. When it did, we reported to the person in charge of filling vacant positions. That was the first time we had any idea what jobs were available. He said that most of the jobs were labor ammunition handlers, with a starting pay of ninety-eight cents per hour. The other jobs were labor in the general supply area, loading and unloading trucks and keeping warehouse floors clean, with a starting pay of ninety-five cents per hour. All jobs were five days a week, eight hours a day regular time, from 8 a.m. to 4:30 p.m.

I reported to the Sierra Ordinance Depot as Caleb Cooper. From that point forward, I stopped being Ardist Cooper, Jr., almost 15 years old, and became Caleb Cooper, almost 20 years old. I changed my name out of fear and anxiety of losing the job opportunity. However, after I finished the application process, it became clear to me that the name change wasn't necessary because no one asked me for identification. Once again, my move proved predestined. It was a miracle for a government job not to ask for ID. I belonged in Herlong.

Sixty-five years later, I still remember the orientation very clearly because that was another turning point in my life. Benefits for a civil service employee began after 30 days; then, you earned 26 days of annual leave and 15 days of sick leave per year. Any leave not used in a 12-month period was cumulative. Boy, I felt like I had made it! We were on six months' probation before promotion to permanent employee status. I knew that, after I became a permanent employee, it would take an act of Congress to get me out. I felt the job was so good that I'd be there for life.

After the brief orientation, we all filled out the work application: name, previous address, height, weight, color of eyes, and color of hair. I filled that part out as Ardist Cooper, Jr. Then for age, date of birth, name, and social security number, I was Caleb Cooper. They assigned all but five of us to be ammunition handlers. Once sworn in, we received further instructions for the job. They paid us every other week, totaling 26 paydays per year.

They assigned our barracks, giving us a choice of single room, a room with double occupancy, or a triple room at a different price. I chose the three-bedroom barrack, for which they deducted $8 out of every paycheck. This cost included daily cleaning and making up the bunk, and changing bed linens twice a week. The barracks were automatically steam heated and cooled for the summer, so we didn't have any utility costs. Married men could apply for family housing in 30 days as it became available. We either bought our own food or ate in the cafeteria. There was a little grocery store to buy food, but they allowed no cooking whatsoever in the barracks.

Although this was a government-owned army ordinance depot, I quickly learned about its segregation. It wasn't publicized, but it was obviously practiced by the types of jobs given, the promotions withheld, and the assignment of barracks (for example, colored men were kept in the 200 block). The overall military housing custom back then was "separate but equal."

The rest of the orientation included instructions about what to wear, where to safely park our car if we drove it to work, and where to catch the government bus that took you to your assigned work area. Those of us working in the ammunitions area couldn't carry matches or smoke. Anyone caught violating that rule was immediately terminated.

As I mentioned before, Herlong wasn't much to look at. Everything about the town and surrounding area was bleak. The people weren't sociably lovable either; they made it clear that they didn't like new people in their town—especially not colored folks.

A few years before my arrival, the ordinance depot used to be a military base where soldiers lived. When I arrived, World War II ended and civilians ran the base administration with a commanding officer in charge. The country was swinging back up again and I was one of the blessed people to have a good job. I had a visceral feeling that this was where I'd be able to fulfill my goal. I felt elated and thanked God for this opportunity.

Today, I still thank God for accomplishing that goal.

Chapter 10

Role Reversal

My New Job

Herlong looked like the high desert. It was brown everywhere—brown fields, brown mountains, and brown roads. Sagebrush and rabbit brush added a pale green color in small patches here and there, but it was mostly just brown. In the winter, it got so cold that it snowed. Then, the summers got so hot that you felt like the furniture could melt from the heat. Looking at the brown landscape, it reminded me again of being like Moses delivering the children of Israel out of Egypt. During their journey, they trekked through desert that I imagine must have looked like Herlong.

I held tightly to my goal of delivering my family from Louisiana, especially my father and mother. To me, Louisiana was a land of bondage for colored people. Most of the time, it felt as if there were absolutely no opportunities to develop our minds to their capacity; however, with much difficulty, I always found a small crack in the wall that you could push through.

I moved into Barracks 29 and was proud of my new home in Herlong. It represented my second home as an independent, responsible adult. My roommates were Abe and Herman. Abe was an ex-army soldier and kind. When I first met him, he said some encouraging words that instantly put me at ease. He was courting a lady in Herlong, so we didn't see him much. Herman was about 20 or 22 years old, also from Oakland. Herman was always friendly and we got along very well.

January 17, 1947 was my first day as an ammunition handler—14 years, nine months and two days old. I walked from my barracks to catch the bus (sometimes a two and one-half-ton truck), which dropped us off in our work area. Once at the job, we didn't need much instruction. We learned by watching the experienced workers. Trained by my dad to learn by watching others, I picked up the daily routine within days: loading, cleaning, and unloading ammunition from trucks. My crew contained seven men, five of which were colored. The foreman was white and made it clear that he expected everyone to do his share.

Half the time I worked outside, and then we rotated with the others and worked inside. I didn't mind where I worked—in the storage igloo, or out in the summer heat or winter snow. To me, work was the same no matter where you were. That is, your performance and effectiveness improved as you learned the art that goes with the skill.

A couple of years later, though, during the middle of winter, I was moving ammunition in weather so cold that I could hardly breathe. As I turned to pick something up, my Achilles' tendon tore from the movement – my tendon was that frozen. The pain was intense, but I didn't dare stop working because we coloreds were always so scared of losing our jobs. I forced myself to finish my shift.

Overall, my crew was friendly, but I ran into some who asked questions that I didn't want to answer, such as, "How old are you?" and "Why aren't you in school?" Some questions I didn't mind answering, such as, "Are you a Christian?"

Since leaving home, I still considered myself a Christian, but I hadn't been active in a church group. I eagerly accepted invitations to fellowship and soon became a member of a local church group.

Being involved with church again gave me an opportunity to do church work. For a while, I taught Sunday school, served as an usher, and sang in the choir. I became a part of the family for two deacons. Their families nurtured me, invited me to share their home meals, and taught me to be a responsible person.

From my first day on the job, I committed to do everything they asked of me—and more—because I was eager to become a permanent employee and wished the next six months would pass quickly. By the end of the first month, time couldn't pass fast enough for another reason—my money was nearly gone and I needed that first paycheck.

I decided to write home, letting my family know of my latest adventure. I thought of writing Uncle Ernest, but decided that, if I wrote Mom, she'd let everyone know. For the fourth time, my letter was full of excitement about my new job. I made it sound like this job would solve all of my woes and nothing but brighter days were ahead.

Looking back, I realize that I never thought of how my mom must have worried sick over her son changing jobs so often. She probably attested that to my being so young, and I'm sure she sent many sincere prayers before God in the name of Jesus on my behalf. Although Mom and Dad probably didn't understand why I kept changing jobs, they never questioned me or gave any indication of doubt. If they felt doubt or worry for my vagabond lifestyle, they expressed it through prayer. I'm confident that, through his prayers, Dad hoped my lifestyle would work out well for me.

A Permanent Employee

Time in Herlong passed rapidly. After work, I learned to play softball and basketball, and took up sport fishing. I also learned to hunt and socialize in various young adult groups, putting on entertainment programs for our little community of 3,000 whites, 2,000 coloreds, and 10 military personnel ranking from sergeant first class up to full colonel.

Most of us lived paycheck to paycheck, so few in the community earned enough to own a car. As was the custom, no matter how much you earned, you still dressed neatly at all times. By today's standards, the clothes we wore to work at the ammunition loading area could pass as acceptable office clothes today. In those days, "keeping up with the Jones's" was in order, which meant dressing up in a shirt and tie even when you were just going to a hamburger joint.

Much like anywhere else in mixed society, and not new to me, I faced my share of racist remarks and obvious unfairness no matter how much harder I worked than the white men around me. I did my best to stay focused on my goal, trying not to let their hurtful ways bring me down or derail me from my path. I let myself become preoccupied with greater things, wanting my family to experience a more level field of opportunities in this greener pastureland out west.

The six-month probation soon passed. I spent each day pressing forward with vigorous energy, determined to succeed and learn how to play my next move. When they promoted me to a permanent employee, my soul filled with such joy and song. After they announced the list of men who made permanent status, people passing me on the street gave me a friendly hello, like I was a lucky so and so.

By now, it was late spring in 1947. Becoming permanent required such stringent rules and regulations that I felt secure enough to write Mom, letting her know that my job was stable and I was ready to welcome any of the children who wanted to come work out here. The Sierra Ordinance Depot was continually hiring, so I felt sure they'd find work soon.

When I sent the letter off, I imagined that one or two children would immediately leave to join me. Days passed, then weeks and months—no word. They may have wanted a better life, but they didn't want it bad enough to leave their comfort zone and what they knew so well.

Joined By My Brother

Then, one day, Caleb wrote, saying that he wanted to come right away because he fell madly in love with a lady, Ms. Dorothy. After he earned enough money, he planned to send for her so they could marry and start a family out here. I sent him $50 in traveling money and he arrived at the depot within two weeks.

As soon as he hopped off the train, he told me about all the changes back home, including the description of their new house.

I stopped him short saying, "We'll get back to that conversation later, Caleb. There's temporary quarters for you. You can clean up and we'll get something to eat."

After he settled in, I listened intently to every detail about Dad's new house. After I ran away, Dad had to give up farming because he only had one son left to do the plowing. With his job as a preacher and all of the serious money managing he did over the years, he saved his money and bought enough lumber to build his own house in Monroe—a town about 40 miles from Warden. It was the first home ever owned by the Cooper family.

"Tell me, Caleb. Is it true that they have electric lights? Wall plugs inside the house? An indoor commode?"

He answered yes to everything as I continued disbelieving.

"... and a bowl hooked up to wash your face? A bathtub with hot- and cold-water hookups? A refrigerator in place of an icebox? A gas cooking stove so Mom doesn't have to burn wood to cook?"

Yes, yes, and yes! Dad's house was like a series of historical achievements all wrapped up in one package.

I sat back and let it all sink in—no more pulling out the old #3 tub for baths, heating the water on the wood-burning stove, sharing dirty bath water, pumping water from the well, unhooking the wash pan from the wall, or filling it with cold water to wash your face. Now, my family walked to a basin and got hot water from a tap! The new house seemed so luxurious compared to my up-bringing, I wanted to see it for myself.

"Caleb, is Mom still doin' the washing on a washboard?"

"Yes, she is."

"Well, I'm going to the Sears store and buy her a washing machine and they will deliver it from the Monroe store."

The day that Mom received her wringer-type washing machine still remains one of my lifelong joys.

After catching up with Caleb, we got down to the serious business.

"Caleb, we need to talk. You will be puttin' in your application Monday for employment. I'll get right to the point. I was very young when they hired me—I'm still not even 16. I thought they would ask for proof of age, so Mom told me your date of birth and I used it and your name. They know me as Caleb Cooper at the depot. If I hadn't been afraid, I could've used my own name because they never asked for any proof. Well, it's done now. You'll need to use my name and any date of birth. Use yours if you want to; they don't know we're brothers."

We pondered the situation for a while, hoping to find a better answer to this identity problem, but knew that falsifying employment applications was serious business—how serious, we didn't know, but we understood enough to keep quiet.

After much thought, it seemed like something short of magic would allow guilty Ardist and contributor Caleb to switch our names back without me losing my job and him losing any chance of getting a job at the depot. Based on that, and with some reluctance on Caleb's part, we agreed that it was necessary to continue our reversed identities.

The next morning, Caleb submitted his application as Ardist Cooper, Jr. They never drafted Caleb during World War II, so he couldn't get the automatic hire status they gave to veterans. The deferment Dad and The Boss were trying to get before I left Warden had passed somehow. I don't know the exact details, but I believe there was a rule that a farmer my dad's age could keep one chief plowboy. Since I was gone and the other boys were too little, Caleb escaped the draft.

Nonetheless, all went well with the application but, before the office could add him to the payroll, he needed to take a physical examination. Unfortunately, his blood pressure was high, so they put him on a waiting list to see a doctor. In the meantime, they suggested Western Pacific Railroad since they were hiring and their office was close. Thinking about the lady in his life, Caleb applied at the railroad and got the job. Their bunkhouse was a short distance from the Sierra Ordinance Depot, which ended up being a good thing.

Two weeks after he started his new job, I came home to my barracks after work and found Caleb standing there.

"What's wrong? No job?"

He spoke in the usual slow, southern manner.

"Boy, I *quit* that job! It's hard and heavy duty."

"Well, what are your plans, Caleb?"

He wanted to retake the physical exam at the depot, which sounded good to me. He went straight to the personnel office, where they set up an immediate appointment, and this time he passed. Two days later, he reported for work as an ammunition handler at a different worksite than mine. We felt so much joy in having jobs that we could have shouted it for the world to hear.

Ms. Dorothy

In a short period, Caleb became acquainted with many of the ladies. Out in the sagebrush, off the depot grounds, several colored-owned clubs housed ladies of the night. These women and their pimps came into Herlong on the weekends, trying to entice men into their clubs that we called the "Do Drop In" or the "Hole in the Wall."

No matter how these ladies tried to get Caleb's attention, or how many local women talked to him, Caleb's conversation and interest always centered on Ms. Dorothy. He was so madly in love with her and set in his mind that she was the girl he was going to marry. He wrote her nearly twice a week for months.

By the third month, he told me, "I'm gonna send for my lady."

"Are you sure that's a good idea? We're workin' under exchanged names!"

We talked briefly about the timing, but Caleb was so eager to marry his love that all of our conversations ended with him sending Ms. Dorothy $75 for train fare and a letter saying, "Baby, won't you hurry and come to me!"

Days went by with no response; then, two to three weeks passed. Finally, a heart-breaking letter came, and each word hurt him like a sharp knife piercing his mind. I sat quietly and listened to him explain the contents of the letter. Caleb spoke louder and louder as he went on.

"She say, 'I got me another man' and 'we were married last week.' She kept the money because I was so long sending for her."

Then the worst came out.

"She also say, 'You know the guy I am married to. He was in our class in school. He was trying to court me then.'"

Caleb took his time swallowing that bitter pill of heartbreak. I wasn't any comfort because I said clumsy things.

"Well, Caleb, things like this happen. May be for the best she didn't come."

Looking back, I realize that it was a terrible thing to say to a brokenhearted person.

In time, Caleb's heart mended. Thanks to my friends, who instantly treated Caleb as a friend, the good-timing women of the town, and the ladies of the evening, Caleb moved on.

From this experience with Ms. Dorothy, Caleb and I formed an unwritten alliance, influenced by the teachings of Mom and Dad, which stated two beliefs: (1) when one person hurts, we all hurt; and (2) let the past stay the past, like water poured in the sand.

That's another one of our old country sayings, "like water poured in the sand." I said it to myself many times since. It helped me keep movin' on, no matter how upset I felt.

Our 1939 Chevrolet

We decided to move forward by planning a trip back home to see our other brothers and sisters. My first order of business was writing Dad, asking for permission to visit. I may have felt like an independent adult at the time, but I always knew who was in charge of my dad's house. Out of respect, I couldn't show up without permission after running off the way I did four years ago. All these years, I communicated through Mom. Asking Dad for permission was a sign of respect. The request was short: I simply asked if it was okay to visit. He said yes.

Months later, Caleb and I accumulated enough leave time. We pulled our money together and purchased a 1939 Chevrolet for the trip. I thought we were hot stuff having our own car. I didn't know how to drive but was determined to learn. How could I own a car and not drive it?

I walked up to Caleb, stuck out my chest and said, "I want the key. I'm goin' for a drive."

"Boy, you don't have a license!"

I reminded him we were out in the desert, so I'd be fine if I stayed on the back roads. He eventually agreed. After a few practice runs, I learned how to hold the car, staying evenly on my side of the road. Then, I got too confident and sped up—being "gas happy," as Caleb called it. Being gas happy was how I learned that our old Chevy was top heavy, so when I went around curves too fast, it flipped over and fell on its side.

The first time Caleb saw the car on its side, he said, "It look like a possum when you come upon an old hollow log and kick it. The possum crawls out and rolls over."

The Chevy fell over three times before I figured out how to slow down enough for the turns. Each time it fell, we never had a dent or broken window. Amazingly, we never got hurt even though cars didn't have seatbelts back then.

One time I flipped over when I was taking Caleb to the doctor in nearby Susanville. He was in a lot of stomach pain and I wanted to get him to the doctor quickly. I forgot about slowing down on the corners and, as we came around a mountain bend, the car flipped over but didn't lay all the way flat. It sat up on its wheels, leaning against the mountainside. We pushed it back on all four wheels and continued, frightened but unhurt.

Chapter 11

Deliverance

Going Home

After our frightening late-evening rush to Susanville, Caleb soon recovered and was back at work. My focus returned to my first visit home since running away four years prior. Although we bought a car for the trip, our 1939 Chevy broke down so many times around town that we decided not to drive it home. Adding to our troubles, it didn't look like Caleb would get vacation time soon, so we postponed our trip home until we could buy a more reliable car. This setback saddened us, but we hoped we could see the family in about six or eight months, at the latest.

A few months later, an unexpected opportunity came up. Since starting in Herlong, I became good friends with one of the workers on my crew, Merwin, and his family, who all came from Arkansas before moving to Herlong. One day, we talked about our families back home and I told him about my desire to see the folks. He said that he was planning to see his grandparents, who lived fairly close to Monroe, and that I could ride with him. He'd drop me off and then pick me up three days later. What a blessing! I immediately sent word: Ardist, Jr., was coming home at last!

I paid for most of the gas during our trip (a gallon of gas cost around twenty-seven cents at that time), and it was less than $40 total. The ride was nice in Merwin's Pontiac, whose slogan was, "Dollar for dollar, you can't beat a Pontiac!" In those days, the speed of cars dictated speed limits. We didn't have any freeways, only two-lane highways where the road was all yours until you slowed down to pass through a small town. Those towns survived on drivers stopping by to eat, gas up, or do a little shopping.

We drove nearly nonstop, only pausing to use the toilet or gas up. To save money and time, we packed our eats in the car. Going full speed like that, it took two full days and nights to reach Monroe. That was a long journey for me, although it was exciting, too. The scenery was marvelous and as uplifting as the song, "Get Your Kicks on Route 66."

However, when we crossed the Mason-Dixon Line, the police stopped us numerous times, using the "N" word when asking where we were going. We knew how to respect them and their unlimited power, saying, "Yes, sir!" and "No, sir!"

Once again, I saw signs separating colored and white for bathrooms, drinking fountains ... *everything*. I thought, "Yes, Cooper, you are back in the South again."

My heart sank a little as I felt the familiar oppression of my past, but those unpleasant reminders were all worth enduring to embrace my family and friends again.

During the car ride to Monroe, I feared the subject of my running away would come up and I would never quite know how to answer it. Nothing sounded remotely believable no matter how I rehearsed the imagined questions. Although my answers would always be the truth, I knew they would be difficult for my parents to believe. My actions were so out of my character because I always wanted to remain with family and didn't have enough self-esteem to entertain adventures.

I silently repeated the answers to my imagined questions about why I ran away. I told no one, no family member had a clue that I was going to run away, and no one helped me or gave me any ideas on where to go. The only thing I could say for sure was I was safely in the hand of Jesus, and my guardian angel directed me, step by step. These answers played over in my head for over 2,000 miles.

As I went over the answers, an inner voice asked, "Is this believable?"

When the Pontiac pulled up to our house, my sisters and brothers ran towards us in welcome. Dad sat on the porch in his usual manner and Mom ran out of the kitchen full of happiness and tears. Four years passed since I ran away from home. Mom and Dad didn't say it, but I could tell they were glad I was alive and well. Although Caleb was nearly 21 years old when he left home, I still feared that Dad would resent his leaving to join me. In fact, Dad never showed any resentment towards Caleb's leaving or my sudden departure years ago.

Dad didn't give me a warm reception, but he welcomed me in his usual southern way, "Hi. How you doin'?"

Men back then didn't show much emotion.

I excitedly gave the family a report on Caleb, saying that he was working and we were both holding our own, humbly adding, "For whatever that's worth," out of respect for my dad. I played with my sisters and brothers, so happy to be with all of them again. Each of their never-ending questions about California started another discussion, which led to more questions.

"How do whites treat coloreds?"

"Can coloreds eat in the same restaurant with whites?"

Then Mom gave her famous call to the table: "This bread is *ready*!"

As usual, there was more food than the whole gang could ever eat. I missed Mom's cooking so much, and I couldn't eat enough that day. Everything Mom cooked was the best I ever tasted. Today, if someone asked what dish I missed most of hers, I'd say, without hesitation or exaggeration, "Everything!"

I felt the familiar comfort of gathering around the table with my sisters, brothers, and parents as we bowed our heads. Dad sat at the head of the table, gave thanks to God, and then each of us followed with our custom of saying a Bible verse. We ate and ate until the thought of hunger was gone. Traditionally, we ate quietly, and then socialized after the meal; we never ate and talked at the same time. Occasionally, though, Dad would discuss something during mealtime or tell a joke, but he was the only one talking and we did the listening.

I spent a considerable amount of my visit in the presence of my mom and dad. We talked about many things, from Uncle Ernest to church and school. We never mentioned anything about why I ran away. All of my worry and practice while driving down to Monroe was for nothing. The Lord Jesus Christ, who does all things well, helped and guided me. My parents never asked why I ran away.

The third day came quickly. We said goodbye with many tears and sad faces as I loaded my bag and headed back to the "wild west" along Route 66. Once on the road, Merwin's family and I shared our joyful experiences. The trip back to the barracks took longer than going to Louisiana because, without the excitement to fuel us, we needed to stop several times for sleep breaks. Whites did not allow blacks to rent motel rooms back then, so we slept on the side of the road. At that time, many white and colored travelers did this because it was safe enough and they would rather save the money.

Years later, when coloreds could rent rooms in small, cheap, back-alley motels, I was driving to Louisiana on my own and got so tired that I decided to get a room. When I tell you that I'm here by the grace of God, I mean it.

I got my key from the office manager and, when I opened the door to my assigned room, I saw a man kneeling down, facing the door with his family behind him. Whether he was kneeling on his weapon or thinking about what he was going to do next, I don't know. I didn't stick around long enough to find out.

As soon as I saw him, I shut the door and ran back to the front office. I gave the office manager back his key, shouting, "Man, you gave me a key with somebody in the room!"

I didn't wait for his answer or a refund. I got back in my car and on the road and rushed out of the state. That incident scared me so furiously that I couldn't calm down for hours.

Can you imagine what could have happened? That man seemed ready to protect his family. He could have wiped me out right then and nobody would have ever known the truth. My family and friends would have to live with the story the papers would tell, which, according to my mental prognosis, would have been "a black man, breaking into a motel room, was killed by the occupants."

I was so scared from that close call that to this day, I can't remember what state I was in at the time. What I can tell you for sure is I drove all the way home without getting sleepy. Soon after that incident, the interstate commerce passed a rule allowing coloreds to rent rooms in the bigger motels and hotels. But I never did. When I got sleepy, I pulled over and slept on the side of the road.

Back to the Barracks

The trusty Pontiac delivered us all back safely. I thanked Merwin and his family several times for allowing me to ride with them, then quickly dropped off my things and ran to where I knew I'd find Caleb. We walked back to Barracks 29 together, and I gave my report on how welcomed I felt on my first trip back to Dad's house since running away.

"Caleb, it was like hitting a grand slam home run!" Having hit many of those on the field, I knew he could relate to that feeling.

I continued, "Everyone appeared to be in good health, and I thank God for that. Man, that house is outta sight! It's everything you said and so much more, compared to the little shotgun house on the farm. It was like a whole new world!"

After my reminder of how whites treated coloreds south of the Mason-Dixon Line, I felt more determined to get the rest of the family out west—especially with the depot hiring every month. Seeing my excitement, Caleb reminded me of the reality.

"You know that Dad won't leave Louisiana, especially with his new house. He don't have to plow now. The mule has been retired."

I was too happy with my own dreams for them, I didn't really listen. "Well, we'll see. Micah's still in the army, but when they release him in a few months, he may wanna come out this way. When you answer his letter, let him know that Herlong is a place for employment."

Three months later, Micah arrived in Herlong. We hadn't seen each other since his last leave before I ran away. He wasn't sure how well I was doing or what I was doing with myself, so he came to check out the situation. He was so displeased with the desert that it took him several days before deciding to apply for work. As a veteran, they accepted his application immediately but tried to keep him from the job he wanted.

He was a very talented auto mechanic in the army (serving with the Tuskegee Airmen) and wanted to continue being a mechanic, but the personnel office said that there weren't any openings at that time. They said that there was an opening for an ammunition handler and they would call as soon as a mechanic position opened up.

Micah was furious. He saw right through their lie but remained calm enough to ask the personnel officer an obvious question, "Why is there a mechanic job on the vacancy board if there are no jobs?"

The personnel officer gave him a dissatisfactory answer. Micah asked to see the military officer, who was a lieutenant colonel in charge of maintenance. He heard Micah's complaint, followed up, and rectified the matter by telling the personnel officer to hire Micah as an auto mechanic.

Micah became the first colored civilian mechanic hired in Herlong and the second colored employee in the mechanic shop. This was the first known victory challenging the staff's biased decisions. Micah worked so well as a mechanic that, within a few months, his fellow workers and the shop foreman accepted him as a person who knew his job well.

The Three Coopers and Aaliyah

After the customary 30 days, Micah applied for family quarters to accommodate his wife and children. Within a month, his family moved in. We three brothers were always together doing church activities or socializing. Friends called us Big Cooper (Micah), Middle-size Cooper (Caleb), and Little Cooper (me)—not because of how old they thought we were, but by our sizes when we stood next to each other. The nicknames followed us all through our years in Herlong.

We participated in uplifting events and sponsored a well-known spiritual group called the Four Pilgrims, making us well known through our many community activities. Although we were together often, we also adopted our individual hobbies: Big Cooper liked working on cars, and Middle-size Cooper and I liked fishing. The fishing was good—not that we caught fish each outing—but the active effort in trying to catch a fish was challenging and fun.

As time passed, my older sister Aaliyah reached 18 years old, married the boy she'd known through high school, then they moved in with his parents. She wanted to join us in Herlong, so we three Coopers agreed to send for them and I put up the money.

Within a few weeks, the Sierra Ordinance Depot employed Scotty, our new brother-in-law, as a laborer in the general supply area. Seeing so much family around me, I felt that my goal of deliverance was materializing. As proud as I was about achieving my goal, my dad quietly disagreed with me. He never stopped anyone from going and never said anything, but I learned much later that he thought it was wrong of me to pull family out of Louisiana. I am satisfied in my belief that, before his days ended on Earth, he realized that the ones who moved west lived a better life.

As the colored population grew in Herlong, friction between whites and coloreds were low key. I believe it was because both groups were happy in their situation. The whites were determined to keep colored employees in inferior positions, and they did so by making all of the decisions in their administrative jobs. We colored didn't mind because we were happy to get jobs of any status and, so long as these jobs paid more than the jobs we held back home, we weren't going to complain. The situation wasn't ideal, but each side felt they had a bigger piece of the pie than they had before. Because of that, we all got along decently.

Chapter 12

What's in a Name?

Confusing Situations

The saying goes, "If one thing isn't troubling you, it's another." For the United States, that something else was the North Koreans. It was 1950 and America was concerned about how crazy the Koreans were acting. The draft boards issued an announcement that all men 18 and older must register immediately if they hadn't already. I wasn't quite 18 years old, but my employer thought I was. They also thought I was Caleb Cooper, who had registered with the draft board in Louisiana. My problem was that Caleb couldn't register for me as Ardist, and Ardist Cooper, Jr., needed to register.

What was I supposed to do?

After much thought, the answer came to me as clearly as the light of day: I'd register as Ardist Cooper, and then give my date of birth as two years earlier to April 15, 1930. Once again, I was grateful that we didn't have computers available to check the facts easily. In those days, we relied on each other's word, and that system worked well because most people kept their word. In business, if someone promised to pay you a certain amount by a certain date, it was as solid as any written contract.

Even with the draft situation settled, I couldn't rest. Once again, if one thing isn't troubling you, it's another. This time it was our 1939 Chevy. That car gave us nothing but trouble from the first day and it kept breaking down no matter how much Micah worked on it. Finally, Micah and Caleb decided to trade the car in for a 1941 maroon Pontiac. The gearshift was by the steering wheel and it looked so modern and sleek. I felt as if we were moving on up! The car didn't have air conditioning because that was still a special order back then, but owning a car—almost any car—was big stuff since most people didn't have one. At that time, I was under the false cloud that what you owned determined your worth. Sitting in our car, I felt 10 feet tall. I'd shine that car every time I saw a little dirt on it. Boy, that car was beautiful, and I was proud of it!

Returning to the South

With the new, supposedly more reliable car, Big Cooper, Middle-size Cooper, and I decided that it was time to go home for a visit. As soon as Caleb and I got our two-week vacation leave approved, we got word that my father's mother passed.

Micah didn't get his leave, so Caleb and I figured out how we could get to Monroe in record time without getting lost. We learned that Highway 80 ran from San Diego, California, straight to Monroe, known as the "southern route." Everything moved smoothly until we travelled 50 miles into Texas—the state that never ends. That state felt like the longest state in the world because our good-looking Pontiac began to give us trouble.

When the gas tank dropped to about half full, the car slowed to nearly crawling and sputtered like it was running out of gas. We pulled off to the side of the road to let it rest; after a while, the car started up again without a problem. Not willing to risk getting stuck, we pulled into the nearest garage, hoping to fix it. After a quick look, the mechanic said that everything was okay. He took our money and we took off. Before long, the whole routine started over again. Each stop cost us from $5 to $10 just to hear nothing was wrong. Back then, $5 was a lot of money and all of those stops nearly used up everything we saved for the trip.

We worried that we'd run out of money for the trip home. Since all of these stops took so much time, we also worried we wouldn't make it home in time for the funeral. But two-thirds of the way through Texas, it seemed as if the car had pity on us and started to run, as it should. Our hearts lifted for it seemed that we were going to make it home in time after all.

Feeling confident again, we rolled through one of the small Texas towns, thinking we looked very cool. A police officer pulled us over, which immediately made us nervous. Even though we weren't speeding, we knew the mentality of the South regarding a couple of colored men driving with California plates.

As usual, the police shouted, "Nigger, *get out of the car!*"

We got out and were very polite and quiet while the police asked their usual questions.

"Where are you going?"

"Is this your car?"

While explaining that we were on our way to our grandmother's funeral, they searched the car and found a gun in the glove compartment. It wasn't illegal to carry a gun back then, and it was common to carry a gun on road trips; however, that didn't stop the police from immediately arresting us, seizing the gun, and handcuffing us both before shoving us into the police car.

We were stuck in jail until our court hearing the next morning at 11 a.m. The police knew that Grandmother's funeral was the same day they arrested us, but they still made us stay the night. All of this time, we had no means of calling home to explain what happened, which was a double whammy for my dad going through the sadness of the funeral while worrying about his two missing boys.

At the hearing, the judge asked where we were going. We gave the same answer we told the police. He asked why we had a gun and we answered truthfully that it was because we were traveling this long distance across country. The judge admitted that he didn't know the charge, but still charged us $15 each before returning our gun and letting us go.

Knowing the mentality of southern police, the family remained worried until we finally arrived. There was great joy when they saw us and heard our testimony.

It took a little while to settle our frustration over missing the funeral, but we finally accepted that the missed fortune was in the past, like water poured in the sand. We could not reverse the event and had four days left to enjoy time with our family. We went to our home church—Palestine Missionary Baptist—for a soul-reviving homecoming. We knew most of the attendees and listened to our old preacher. We spent time on the creek bank fishing, but not for sport because this was serious business. We had to catch more than enough for our customary family fish fry. Oh, how we loved to eat fish!

The shortest time in one's life appears to be when you are enjoying what you are doing. Looking back, all of our trips were so short because it took at least six days to drive home and back if we drove nonstop. Looking back, I realize we didn't have to rush. We could have spent more time enjoying family because, as civil service employees, we all received 25 days of vacation time. However, we colored were always so scared of losing our jobs that we didn't dare take all of that time off. Our supervisors made us feel that, if we left for more than two weeks, we were putting the entire operation in a bind, so we didn't fuss. I don't regret much in life, but I do regret not using more of our assigned vacation time to see my parents more in those earlier years.

Our four days were nearly over when we received two requests to journey back west with us: my mother's brother, Paul, and Becky, a slightly older lady whom Caleb met. Becky's dad was working in Herlong at the time. They met us on the day of departure and we all packed the car once again, saying our goodbyes through many hugs and tears.

Caleb and Becky

We returned to Herlong without any serious delays or car troubles. Once home, we took our car into a mechanic in Reno. The mechanic quickly figured out the problem and fixed it for only $1.50! He said if the trouble started up again, he'd return our $1.50 because the "problem" was a malfunction in the design of the gas tank floater. He took it out and, sure enough, that fixed the problem.

Uncle Paul didn't care much for Herlong. In fact, he really didn't make any effort to adjust to the new land. He stayed around for a week, looking the place over, before we drove him to Oakland to visit his brother, Uncle Ernest. He stayed there for a weekend, and then decided to head back to Louisiana. A couple of months later, he moved to Houston, Texas.

During this time, Caleb and Becky became more intimate. Within three months of returning to Herlong, they got married without telling anyone. They drove to Reno, Nevada, one day, tied the knot, and started their new life together. Caleb applied for family housing on the depot, which was the only housing within 34 miles. They had to wait 15 days before a family housing vacancy became available, so they lived with her dad and stepmom until then.

The only problem with their marriage was that Caleb and I still kept each other's switched names at work. Caleb showed me the paperwork where he applied for family housing under the name Ardist Cooper. He swore that our secret would be safe with Becky and that we needed to tell her. I agreed, but neither of us could foresee how other people would eventually learn about our secret.

Becky got into the habit of calling her husband "Caleb" in public. This confused our friends who always knew him as Middle-size Cooper or Ardist. It didn't take long for rumors to spread. Some would ask us questions, and we always had the same answer, "Well, I guess we should know our own name!"

Most people let it drop, calling us Big Cooper, Middle-size Cooper, and Little Cooper. Still, it only took a few months for the gossip to reach the ears of the Sierra Ordinance Depot administrators. The person in charge of investigating fraud called me into his office.

"Is what I've been hearing about you and your brother true? You all switched names?"

We'd ask surprised, "Sir, who would tell you somethin' like *that*?"

"I cannot give you my source of information."

Then I asked, "Sir, do you have an idea what would be the need for us to switch names?"

He couldn't answer and let me go for the time being.

I rushed back to Caleb, letting him know what happened. A few weeks later, the investigator summoned Caleb and asked him the same questions. Caleb gave primarily the same replies I gave earlier. The investigation was quiet for the next four months, and then something got out about our name change. The investigator called us back in, sure that he had the goods on us and that he could terminate our employment.

Caleb and I sat in different rooms while the investigator questioned me and his assistant questioned Caleb. We had a strong defense.

"If you have information," we said, "put it on the table. If you're pressin' me by relying on statements from someone else, bring those people forth."

We didn't rehearse our reply, but we ended up saying the same thing and that was enough to put a damper on the questioning for a while longer.

I firmly believe the investigator couldn't build a case against us because God was helping us. God blinded their thinking, causing the investigator to forget to look up birth records or drivers' licenses. Now if that statement doesn't convince you that the Lord Jesus Christ held back the night, then read on…

Do you remember how I registered for the draft? That made the situation more confusing for the investigator. Caleb received his "Greetings from the President" letter, summoning him back to serve in the army. He told me that he would report for duty under his true name Caleb Cooper. When I heard that, I paniced and I prayed, "Man, oh man! The investigator will be back, asking questions for sure! Come here, angel. Tell me what to do before the depot finds out about our name switch!"

Stress nearly doubled me over at that time because I was so afraid of losing my job. I also had another reason to keep my job:

Joan, the girl whom I was courting at that time, was raising our two children. We had a boy and a girl, who were living with Joan's aunt nearby the depot. I secretly saw them every day and wanted to marry Joan, but how could I get married without all those people at work finding out my real name?

The fear kept saying to me, "When you lose your job, how you gonna support a wife and children?"

That fear didn't paralyze me; instead, it ignited my self-determination. I took a week of annual leave to enlist in the army under my true name, Ardist Cooper, Jr., thinking that this would correct the fraud. To my surprise, I had to pass a written test to be a volunteer soldier. I tried every recruiting station in Reno, Nevada, trying to get into the army, navy, and marines, but I couldn't pass any of the written tests.

I was so depressed and blamed everyone I could think of for my inability to pass the tests. I travelled to Sacramento, visiting every recruiting office again. I returned to the army office twice. The second time, they suggested that I was too nervous and, if I calmed down, I would pass. I failed the test a third time. Once again, I blamed everyone else for my situation. I didn't want to admit that I was the only one to blame. I was the one who dropped out of school in the fourth grade.

"Greetings from the President"

My head hung very low. I felt like it was the saddest day of my life when I boarded the Greyhound bus back to Herlong. I felt totally defeated and drained. At 17 years old, I believed that my life was over. I wish I knew then what I know now: When your mind reaches overload like that, it needs quiet prayer time.

Prayer time lets you reach back in your experience and look at Jesus Christ's record. I am confident of the fact that during my heavy burdens, Jesus showed me the way through. I am a living testimony that, if the Lord Jesus had not been on my side, I could not have survived. The Lord Jesus has His plan, and He will work it in spite of your trying and stumbling. During the bus trip home,

I finally remembered all of this and realized that the solution of getting into the armed services was already worked out ... I just didn't know it yet.

By the time I reached Herlong, my mind and body settled down. My roommate left mail on my bunk, so I flipped through it. That's when I saw the most uplifting letter that all my soul could handle: "Greetings from the President of the United States." I was glad my roommate wasn't there because I barely kept myself from shouting all over the place! Me of little faith wasted five days, trying to solve an already-solved problem. I didn't have to pass a written test after all, which was a relief. When I told people that they drafted me, some were sad.

I'd answer, "Someone has to go."

I didn't tell them how hard I tried to enlist just a few days before. I was so thankful for the greetings that I didn't give any thought of my possible death. I knew there was a serious battle going on in Korea and a good chance that they would ship me over there, but my focus was on getting married. I told Joan as soon as I got in the army and got a pass that I was coming to marry her.

Soon, I boarded the bus with 70 other new recruits. I was probably the youngest of the group with the most grown-up experiences. We boarded the troop bus in Susanville on March 14, 1951, heading to Fort Ord. Our first eating stop was in Reno. Our troop had 68 whites, one American Indian, and me. When we arrived in Reno, we filed out of the bus into the restaurant. Without thinking, I sat at the front counter with the other recruits.

The waitress immediately walked over, looked at me, and said, "If you want to eat, you need to go to the back table."

Boy, that hurt me so badly! You have no idea how deep those words hurt. I turned around, without saying a word, and sat inside the bus. The GIs felt sorry for me and offered to get me a sandwich, but I was too hurt to eat.

By now, the other GIs were getting used to me enough to start thinking, "Hey, this colored guy ain't so bad"; however, that type of racism was common back then. So when an incident like the one in the restaurant happened, the GIs stared straight ahead without saying anything. They weren't supporting it, but they weren't speaking up against it either. Up until that time, I forgot about being colored. I was a soldier like the others—all of us willing to lay down our lives for our country. That waitress harshly reminded me that I wasn't equal. Not wanting to be humiliated again, I stayed on the bus all the way to Fort Ord, never getting off when the others stopped to eat.

Down the Aisle

By April 22, 1951, I was trained enough to get a weekend pass. I kept my word to my girl, got on a bus to San Francisco airport, and flew from San Francisco to Reno. Joan met me there to stand before the judge and say, "I do."

Right after the ceremony, they dropped me back to the airport and I flew back to San Francisco. I was afraid of reporting to Fort Ord late because we weren't supposed to be that far from base on a weekend pass; however, like the rest of my life, I took the chance. This chance was the most important because it meant keeping my word.

I didn't let my friends and family know about my plans until after I got married. I knew they'd think I made an irrational decision because I may not come back from Korea. The way I see it is everybody has opinions, but you just have to do what you're going to do.

The only thing I cared about was that my family had security if I didn't come back from the war. At that time, my son was 18 months old and my daughter was four months old. They didn't vote to come; it was my responsibility to give them a fair life. Once married, Joan would get an allotment from the government to live on and feed the children. I started the allotment and, in a reasonable time, she began to receive assistance. Because we were married, I felt peace knowing that the military would treat my children as a veteran's kids and have a chance to go to school and succeed.

Chapter 13

Being a Soldier

Army Training

After my shotgun wedding, I completed six weeks in basic combat training at Fort Ord, Company F of the 63rd Infantry Regiment. During this time, the new recruits passed around stories, saying that they would ship us out to the front lines and we'd likely never come back. Some of us knew these were rumors, but many of us feared they could be true. Basic training was a learning experience that I'll never forget. It was partly because, as we learned, we did so knowing the information could save our life, our fellow soldiers, and our country. This wasn't school; this was survival.

The army trained us to think and act defensively with our new best friend: the M1 rifle. We carried it everywhere—practicing, eating, and sleeping with it. It weighed about nine pounds but, to us new recruits, it felt more like 99 pounds. The physical as well as the emotional weight of knowing that you may use it against a fellow human being made the rifle heavy.

Joan and I communicated by letter while I trained in Fort Ord and then transferred to Fort Bliss in Texas. The whole Company F rode to Texas on a troop train, and then rode military trucks from the train station to the army base. There, they assigned us to Battery D, which was a light artillery unit. We spent the next eight weeks learning how to operate Quad 50 caliber machine guns, mounted on top of a half-track (an armored, tank-like vehicle).

For firepower efficiency, the vehicle held a scope man, the driver, and one gunner, with an ammo bearer on the right and left of the gunner to feed the ammo. The 37mm weapon, whose shells could be used for aircraft destruction, mounted on the vehicle as a component unit. The 40mm weapon was more powerful than the 37mm and had a longer range. It could also be used for aircraft destruction, and was mounted on its mechanism, like a cannon, ready to be set, stabilized, and then concealed from aircraft.

We trained vigorously to use these weapons, rifles, and bayonets, and studied hand-to-hand combat techniques. When we weren't training, we worked guard duty, which meant walking our post in a military manner, keeping on the alert, and observing everything taking place within sight or hearing. We had 12-hour shifts of four hours on duty, then two hours off. We couldn't leave our post until properly relieved by the Sergeant of the Guard. Once relieved, we rested during the two hours off, but it felt like only 15 minutes passed before the sergeant yelled in our ear, "Soldier, let's go!"

Guard duty was tedious, but it was better than being on kitchen patrol, otherwise known as "KP." No matter what position they assigned to you in Fort Bliss, it was serious. You reported for KP at 4 a.m. to peel spuds, wash pots and pans, or wash dishes. If you worked super fast, and the person assigned to you worked super fast, you may get out of there by 9 or 10 p.m.

When you were on KP, your only breaks were making fast trips to the restroom and rushing through your breakfast, dinner, and supper. You had to keep a furious pace the entire 16 hours to get out of there by 10 p.m. The mess hall fed 72 men, officers, and noncommissioned officers. As soon as one meal was over, it was time for the next. Although we all worked KP, I confess that none of the assignments in the kitchen appealed to my ego.

Fort Bliss was huge, like its own town; however, during the first two weeks of training, they confined us to our company area. After that, we received weekend passes to go off base or visit the rest of

Fort Bliss. On base, everyone was treated the same. The commanding officer did not permit racism, but the army didn't have any authority outside the base. Before letting us go, our commanding officer reminded us of a few things.

"You're in the South. Fort Bliss is open to all on an equal premise, but should you go off base and ride the city buses, or patronize the restaurants or service clubs, respect the civilian laws and customs."

Everything went smoothly until some time before our third weekend pass came around. They ordered the entire battalion to dress in their Class A uniform and assemble before the battalion commander. We learned that some colored soldiers challenged a bus driver, who told them to get in the back of the bus, and the army had an effective way for controlling its troops.

When someone disobeyed rules, the extra duty was strenuous enough to make you think twice before repeating the offense. One punishment was Article 15, where your commanding officer can dock two-thirds of your pay for six months. If something happened where no one knew the guilty party, the entire battalion was restricted to their company area for weeks or even months. While we assembled the battalion in our Class A uniform, our commanding officer reviewed the offense, named the offenders, and announced the punishment. That reminder kept us all out of trouble for our remaining six weeks there.

My time in Fort Bliss passed swiftly. I'm proud to report that the training made me strong in my weapons knowledge and prepared me to perform my duties as a soldier confidently. They gave us a farewell speech on graduation day, and then most of Battery D received a 17-day delay en route to the Far East.

17 Days

By now, they recalled Micah to active duty, stationed in Fort Lewis, Washington; Caleb just finished his training, stationed in Fort Lawton, Washington. I let them know I was driving up to see them before I shipped off.

I felt pretty good about myself as a private E-2 in the U.S. Army, heading home to spend 17 days with my new wife. I was so happy to see her! I sent three letters, saying that I was on my way and it wouldn't be but a few more days.

After each eight-week training session and graduation, cadets and teachers got a short break before a new wave of recruits came in. That's when soldiers took time to make extra money driving new graduates to their various destinations. Many made from $200 to $300 a week doing this, which was a lot of money back then.

I joined a car of five white graduates heading to California—the same guys I was with from Susanville to Fort Ord back in March 14, 1951. The trip started enjoyably. The soldier driving us charged $25 per person, plus gas. It seemed a little pricey, but we all paid it because it was the fastest way to get home and we were short on time. Even though we knew that we were heading to Korea soon, and there were shooting and soldiers killed every day, we discussed great plans for our lives after we returned home. Although we gave reality a little consideration, we tried to focus on how we would enjoy the next 17 days.

It was the first time I rode through the South in a car with a bunch of white men. The trip was smooth because of it, until we stopped for lunch at one of the Texas cafeterias. We all walked into the cafeteria and seated ourselves. Two waitresses came to our table, talking to each other while staring at me.

One asked in her slow, southern drawl, "Should we serve *him?*"

The other said, "Well, I guess we can. He's with *them.*"

Although they served me, it was so awkward that we all agreed to avoid that type of embarrassment again. Our new plan was for the other guys to eat while I waited in the car, and then they'd bring me a sandwich. We followed this plan all the way to California. When we reached Herlong, we couldn't rush out of the car and grab our duffel bags fast enough. We shouted goodbyes as we looked eagerly around for our families.

Joan didn't bring the kids, so we had time to catch up a little. Talking fast, we tried to fill in the details that four months of letter writing didn't cover. We both kept talking at the same time, and didn't understand anything the other person was saying except that we missed each other. I was eager to go home and spend time with my little ones, and see how much they changed over those last four months.

I truly enjoyed my next few days as a husband and father. I was the head of the household and a family man. I felt so happy being with them. Herlong is so small that I easily found time to visit all of my old friends and co-workers.

I also found time to visit Micah and Caleb in Washington. Their bases were only 34 miles apart from each other, so I was able to spend time with them both. We had a grand time together— talking, laughing, and reminiscing about the old days on the farm.

Every so often, the mood grew serious when they thought about me going to Korea. At this point, my orders only stated that I was reporting for FECOM (Far East Command). I tried to calm my brothers' worries by saying what I usually say, "I can handle it."

Then, we lightened the mood again when I told them the safety advice an army major passed onto me: "If you wind up on the front line and the enemy is shooting at you, don't forget to turn sideways so the bullets can pass you by."

When I returned to Herlong, I spent a long evening with my roommates in Barracks 29, especially Abe. He was in every sense a big brother. I also spent quality time with the deacon and his wife, who were my trusted mentors.

Sailing Away

Time doesn't stay still. My next stop was Camp Stoneman, California—the port of embarkation, destination FECOM. While I prepared for the trip, I started to think that Herlong wasn't a good place for Joan and the kids. I felt that she needed the help of friends and family, so I suggested that she stay with my parents in Monroe. She didn't like that idea because she didn't know them, so then I suggested that she stay with her parents in Harvey. She wasn't sure if she wanted to do that either. I left the subject open, saying that it was for her to decide.

The day soon came when Joan and I drove to Camp Stoneman. During the near 300-mile drive, I struggled to hide my true feelings and tried to sound positive. Thoughts were furiously flying around in my head about everything that could go wrong and my uncertain future. I worried about our two children. I worried about Joan. I worried that I wouldn't come back. The closer we got to Camp Stoneman, the more fearful I became, but I didn't say anything to Joan. I'm sure she had similar worries, but didn't voice them. Folks in our time didn't discuss much.

When I arrived, I found the area where I would later ship out, so I mingled with the Battery D troop and their families for a few hours. The army's standard operating procedure, I learned, was to hurry up and wait, but the time finally came to line up and load into the back of a two and one-half-ton truck, heading to the ship. Once loaded on the truck, I sat on my duffel bag, ready to move out, but we sat there for another 10 minutes before the trucks started towards the docks, which were five miles away. As far as I could see, there were endless hands waving farewell. It was both a happy and a sad sight.

Sometime before sundown, I boarded the USS Private Sadao S. Munemori (T-AP-190) to sail the ocean blue waters. The ship was crammed full with 2,700 new recruits and crew bound for Asia. We didn't know for sure where we'd end up. We just hoped that we'd return.

Chapter 14: FECOM

Life on the Ship

A few months after I shipped out of Camp Stoneman, Joan and our two children moved in with her parents back in Harvey, Louisiana, which was a great comfort to me. Once assigned to our bunk on the ship, I felt a deeper understanding of the phrase "packed in like sardines." The officers announced that our next port of embarkation was in Japan; once there, they'd tell us our assignments, and then send us off again.

It took 12 days to reach Japan, but it took me less than an hour to learn that I got seasick. I'd never been on a boat before, and all that rolling and tossing in the water did things to my stomach and made me very dizzy. Believe me, it's one of the worse sicknesses to have.

I found a little comfort in a small New Testament Bible the chaplain handed out as we boarded, to anyone who was interested. I had never read the New Testament from Matthew through Revelation, but I was so scared about going to Korea and so miserable from seasickness that I read that book from cover to cover! It took 12 days to read every word. By the time we docked in Japan, my fear diminished slightly, solely on the assumption that combat couldn't feel any worse than my ocean experience.

Even though many of the GIs on board probably felt as scared as I did, you couldn't tell with all the laughing and storytelling going on. You would think that the ship would be full of seriousness and sadness, but it was full of laughter and games. American soldiers were crazy that way—they were always trying to laugh. Usually, there were so many soldiers in a good mood that we didn't notice the sad ones, or they soon forgot that they were sad and started laughing, too.

In such close quarters, whites and coloreds didn't have much choice but to talk. Many whites never saw colored people before because we just didn't live in their part of the country. Whites heard many stories about coloreds, and they naturally believed them until they talked to one in person.

They asked questions like, "Where's your tail?" and "Does your color rub off?"

Most of them thought that coloreds weren't smart, which isn't true. These men soon realized that not being "learned," due to limited opportunities, was different from not being smart. Some wanted to feel my hair and, when they did, they were usually surprised, "Why, that's not so nappy. It feels softer than I thought."

One of the funniest comments I heard was, "Well, you guys aren't much different than us. You just got left in the oven longer, that's all!"

First Stop: Japan

I leaned heavily on hope over the months ahead. When we arrived in Japan, we boarded trains to an army base about six hours away. During the train ride, we passed Nagasaki and Hiroshima. Both towns still showed evidence of how our atom bombs ended a war not too long before.

After filing out, we zeroed our weapons, which meant firing them to make sure they shot. Then we stood in battalion formation for our briefing. The sergeant announced that the 7th, 24th, and 25th Divisions were going to Korea. They would begin roll call soon to assign our divisions. Those going to Korea would be fighting in the front lines 48 hours from that moment. When I heard that, I forgot about my seasickness as my mind filled up with new fears.

The sergeant tried to boost our courage with a speech, reminding us how we're all well-trained soldiers and can outmaneuver the Koreans. I really wanted to believe him. The colored men started whispering to each other, saying that the 24th and 25th Divisions were reactivated units from World War II, and I heard parts of these conversations.

"Did you hear that the troops are all colored and the officers are all white?"

"The army hasn't fully integrated yet."

"If we get on with the 24th and 25th, at least we'll be with experienced troops."

Before we could count to 10, the whispers stopped and roll call started. When they called your last name, you responded with your first name and middle initial.

The sergeant called, "Cooper!"

"*Ardist, Jr., sir!*"

I was one of the first 100 names called, and we were all colored. We looked at each other and knew where we were going because we heard that they hit the 24th and 25th Divisions hard. There was only one thought going through my head, "Oh, my God. I'm goin' to Korea. Goodbye world!"

We stood around waiting for our marching orders while the other 3,000 men finished roll call. Once we all received our assignments, two-thirds of the troops moved out. Fortunately, they assigned my group of 100 to the Second Logistical Command under General Dodge and Colonel Traylor. It wasn't the hotspot where the 24th and 25th Divisions fought, but it was another hotspot.

General Dodge and Colonel Traylor were the top-ranking officers in the U.N. prisoner-of-war camp in Koje-do Island, and North Korean POWs had just captured General Dodge during a prison uprising. Our orders were to help secure the prisoners until additional troops came. With that briefing, we boarded the ship and sailed to Korea.

Next Stop: Koje-do Island

Koje-do Island was about 20 square miles. They separated more than 70,000 prisoners into compounds, which guards patrolled 24/7. At least two machine gun towers surrounded each compound, and 10-foot barbed-wire fences offered little protection for the guards.

The island held about 250,000 North Korean and communist Chinese prisoners, about 3,000 American soldiers and officers, around 500 rock soldiers (what we called North Koreans at the border), and 50 South Koreans attached to the American army as interpreters and guards. It may seem as if there were many guards, but these were hard-core communist prisoners who always caused trouble. The POW camps had one violent riot after another—it was part of the North Korean strategy to keep more of our soldiers engaged there and off the front lines.

The prisoners lived in Quonset huts, and were given a blanket and clothing and fed daily. Part of their daily work detail was filing out to clean their huts. One day, one of the communist prison leaders called General Dodge to the gate, insisting that he hear their complaints directly. The general and one of his staff, Lieutenant Colonel Razen, stood outside the compound gate, listening to the leader's complaints.

As the men were in deep conversation, the compound gate opened slightly to let the work detail out. A group of prisoners ambushed the officers and dragged them into the barbed-wire enclosure. The guards saved Lieutenant Colonel Razen, but the prisoners took General Dodge hostage. The prisoners had this planned for a while because, when they dragged General Dodge to his hideaway, a little vase with flowers sat on the floor waiting for him. The prisoners knew that they would succeed.

I was in the light artillery unit, which means the weapons we used were 40mm, 37s, and Quad 50s. We were not safe, but we were better off than the infantrymen. When I trained in Fort Ord, I trained as an infantryman; when I trained in Fort Bliss, I trained as a light artilleryman. I learned that a light artilleryman gets a little more firepower, and you are a few seconds behind the infantrymen. Every little advantage helps.

116

When we arrived, we jumped right into the madness. During the fighting and negotiations, the prison leaders spread word from compound to compound. They told the prisoners and the American soldiers about their plan to take over the entire island, made demands, and threatened General Dodge's life. The prisoners got more and more aggressive, thinking they would succeed.

My commander was a major, which meant I could occasionally stand close enough to hear the officers strategize and pass information back and forth. Seeing the apprehensive looks on their faces and hearing their conversations first hand, I felt as if I were an S-2, which was an intelligence officer for the security unit.

This madness continued for six hours until the first backup came. Oh, what a relief! The Fifth Air Force flew overhead for 45 minutes. If you've ever seen a full Blue Angel's show, they simulate the same attack. The Fifth Air Force wasn't bombing or shooting; they were just showing their force to warn the prisoners.

Within 48 hours, at least two companies of the 182nd Airborne landed on the island, followed by the 10th Combat Engineers. They brought in tanks equipped with 90mm guns and half-tracks, carrying 105mm howitzers and flamethrowers to keep the prisoners back. Seeing all that power is enough to demand the respect of anyone.

With air and ground troops backing them up, the Americans quickly regained control of the island. The prisoners kept General Dodge hostage for a total of 78 hours before they released him, unharmed.

Then the combat engineers started to do the serious work. The new general in command, General Conlon, ordered that the prisoners divide into enclosures of 72 men each. In order to prevent another uprising like that from ever happening again, we had to look strong even though we may be weak.

Boy, those combat engineers were something to watch! They sent them right inside the compounds of 50,000 people or more, and then drove their half-tracks with flamethrowers to keep the prisoners back. At the same time, they made smaller compounds by putting up fences within fences, like little rooms. Then they pushed the prisoners back while we kept order as the other soldiers worked.

It was a powerful sight to see so many soldiers working collectively. Watching all of this organized activity reminded me of the Bible's reports:

Nehemiah 4:17 says, "They which builded on the wall, and they that bare burdens, with those that laded, every one with one of his hands wrought in the work, and with the other hand held a weapon," and then Nehemiah 4:18, "For the builders, every one had his sword girded by his side, and so builded."

It showed how the people rebuilt the walls of Jerusalem: Armed men worked, and more armed men watched the enemy as the work continued. This was a big operation, but it only took four months to complete because those combat engineers were professionals!

Koje-do Island ultimately had 3,000 American soldiers and officers, two rock companies, and 144 men including the Korean interpreters. The commanders recognized the need for perpetual backup troop support. They arranged for division units to fall back, train, and then strategize on the island as they rotated off the front lines.

When they sent me to the Second Logistical Command, they sent the other men, whom I trained with in Fort Bliss, to the 24th and 25th Divisions. Two months after I arrived on Koje-do, GIs were rotating off the front lines and came to Koje-Do as reinforcement for us. While chatting with some of the guys, I heard about the casualties. It was only two months and most of them were gone. I thought, "Oh, my God! Already?"

If they weren't gone, the North Koreans shot them. They hit one guy, and the army sent him back to the front lines in just two months. I figured that we were really blessed being in Koje-do. The prisoners took over for a little while, but we got back in control in a hurry.

Seeing our action first-hand, I still tell people—especially our young black boys—that the American army is powerful and they should consider joining. I explain, "Listen, our country may have its faults, but when the chips are down, we know what to do. Why don't you volunteer for the military, get your act together, and go to college?"

They usually say, "No. I ain't going to no military. They fight ..."

I say, "Look, you can do things stupidly, but mostly you'll go when it's your time to go. It doesn't matter where you are. I'm living proof."

Being in a war zone is like life: Either you're going into a storm or you're coming out of one. If you survive, it gives you confidence. That's why so many American soldiers joked, even when we were at the point of death. Joking gave us courage.

Give up-itis and Hope

As a soldier, we felt young and strong, and too alive to think of dying. If we weren't talking about our girlfriend, then we were talking about how we would get married and have 10 kids—anything to keep us going. None of us knew where we were going, but we always talked about what we were going to do when we got back.

I think it's human nature to always think that things are going to be all right, like when you go to see someone who's really, really sick. You know that they don't have much longer, but they still make plans, saying things like, "When I get out of this bed, I'm going to ..."

When you lose that hope, you're a goner for sure.

The Koreans didn't treat American POWs any worse than we got treated in other wars. But according to the Red Cross, more American POWs died in the Korean War than in any of the other wars in America's history. They claimed that it was due to "give up-itis," meaning that the soldiers died, without signs of abuse or poison, because they lost hope. For some reason, they couldn't see a way out and thought they'd be there forever.

I learned about give up-itis later when we were heavily fighting every day.

The commanding officer had us all stand in formation, encouraging us never to give up if captured. He said that our jobs as prisoners were to make as much fuss as possible, so the enemies used more soldiers to guard us. Then, when they were busy guarding us, they were not on the front lines killing our buddies.

My adopted motto alongside numerous other fellow soldiers was, "If I'm going, I may as well go out fighting. If they're gonna take me down, I'm gonna take 'em with me!"

One encouraging element of my time at Koje-do Island was that the wounded and casualties were minimal (if "minimal casualties" is an appropriate saying). Months later, we heard through the grapevine that General Dodge was relieved of his command and busted down to a colonel. General Bodanek, who replaced him, remained on the island another two months before rotating. Rumors spread that he received another star. The soldiers talked about how humiliating it was to lose a star and face mandatory retirement.

Thinking about General Dodge's retirement, we usually stopped feeling sorry for him and said. "I bet he still got the same amount of money!"

CONUS

After each month spent in Korea, I counted my rotation points. Each earned point brought me closer to home, and we needed 24 points to rotate back to CONUS (Continental United States). We earned four points for every month in a combat zone, three points for being between regimental headquarters and emplaced batteries, and two points for rear-echelon duty. With the point system, you could go home in six months if you spent the whole time in the front line—and survived.

As the months went by in the front lines, I experienced many situations where I really thought it was the end for me. Soon, I adopted the same phrases spoken by most of the other soldiers.

"Don't start no long conversation with me. We may not have time to complete it."

"When I get to the pearly gates, if there is any delay in entering into everlasting rest, I surely will tell dear Lord I have spent my hitch in hell. I was very cold in the winter and very hot in the summer."

I was one of the blessed ones. Nine months later, the day finally came when I earned my rotation back to CONUS—my sweet land of liberty, my country.

I looked around the South Korean hills, which were mostly barren. I thought about the few good times—and the many, many challenging and bad times—with my fellow soldiers. I could finally leave it all behind me, but I felt genuine sadness and guilt in my heart. I was leaving behind the memories as well as my fellow soldiers. We became family as we fought side by side, wondering if each hour would be our last.

Along with my sadness and guilt, I felt soul-stirring gratitude and joy when I thought about rejoining my wife and two children. Yes, my country was full of imperfections, but I was returning as an American soldier and I felt good ... *real* good. I was alive! It felt as if years had passed since I saw my mom and dad, and my brothers and sisters. I missed them all and wanted a normal life where I could see my family and work a regular job.

As standard operating procedure, I entered the troop movement lineup, boarded the USS Marine Lynx (T-AP-194), and headed back home. It seemed like the longest journey in history and, to make it worse, I was still seasick. I felt close to death on my journey to Japan, but I felt worse this time because I wasn't scared and instead felt the sickness more intensely.

On this trip, we soldiers had so much experience under our belts that we gave the sailors a hard time, calling them sea-going bellhops who just delivered soldiers to the war zone and took off, floating around the ocean doing nothing. Of course, this wasn't true, but we were ignorant and full of pride.

The ship's captain was a powerful and authoritative man. He stayed out of the squabbles between the sailors and the soldiers all through the trip home; however, on the last day, he gave us all some wisdom, "You soldiers think it's hard to put up with sailors and their mannerisms. Well, it was just as hard for the sailors to put up with your mannerisms."

When the slowest ship in the world finally made its landing in Seattle, Washington, I wanted to act like a hog as soon as my feet touched the ground—just wallow in the mud and thank God for dirt!

It took another four hours for dismissal, assignment to a company assembly area, and briefing on the camp we would be traveling to until our discharge. Those discharged or reassigned had time to make a phone call and move around a little. However, making a phone call was like mission impossible with thousands of happy soldiers eager to call home. Each time I pushed towards the phone, someone squeezed in and grabbed it before me. The feeling was similar to another biblical truth where a man waited 38 years at the edge of a pool (St. John 5:7 "But while I am coming, another steppeth down before me"). He just needed to step in and be healed, but each time he was about to take the step, someone stepped in before him, so he never made it into the pool.

I was in a group returning to Fort Ord for discharge/release on a Douglas C-47 Skytrain, but I asked the major in charge if I could return another way. C-47s were not staying up in the air reliably, and I feared the thought of surviving the front lines for nearly a year and then falling out of the sky on my own soil. The major was courteous enough to say that the only way to avoid it was to get a sick-call exemption from the doctor. Knowing that this process would delay my return home, I swallowed my fear and boarded the plane.

Once on the plane, we soldiers watched as hundreds of people happily welcomed us back home from war-troubled Korea. Some were celebrities, but most were dear, gentle-hearted people who gave us a real hero's welcome. I'm confident in saying I did what I was told and never retreated until ordered to do so. I did a job of which I can be proud.

As we say in the army, though, "The real heroes are the ones left behind."

We landed in Fort Ord three hours later, settled into temporary quarters, and stared at the walls for four days with nothing to do but wait for our discharge/release. They ordered us to get a standard GI haircut and be in our Class A uniform, which we did with quiet impatience.

We returned from a battle in Korea that we didn't win, no matter how hard we tried. Korea was a strange war, and we were frustrated, feeling as if we risked our lives for nothing. It fueled our impatience when we tried to put it all behind us and resume our old life. Trying to push down that impatience made us lose our tempers easily. But we all watched out for each other. When one person felt like voicing his impatience, the others reminded him not to rock the boat. We all knew that, in a few days, they would turn us loose, and we could say, "So long, *sir*!"

On the fourth day, I looked sharp and felt proud when I received that farewell paper. I put it in my duffel bag and headed straight for the Greyhound bus stop within walking distance from base. I was as happy and full of joy to get out of the army as I was to get in it. Boy, that felt like a lifetime ago!

Back to Herlong

I kept that joy in my heart for 106 miles to San Francisco. Once I arrived, I headed to Granada Street to my old friend Sean's house. I knew his family since we were children back home in Warden, Louisiana. His family hadn't heard from me for quite a while and didn't know I was stopping by. It was a very happy reunion, full of laughter and shared stories.

Sean's son asked me if I was still in the army because I was wearing my Class A uniform. I told him no, and reached into my duffel bag to show him what an army discharge looked like, which was the first time I actually looked at the paper. I panicked because it said "release" and not "discharge." I didn't know what that meant, so I called the base, read off the words on the document, and asked if they gave me the wrong paper.

I asked, "Will I get my discharge in the mail?"

The person on the other line calmly explained that I had the correct papers. "You won't get a discharge for two years. We may need you in a few days' notice. That release keeps you in a 'ready for recall' group." (I received my discharge on March 30, 1956.)

I didn't like the idea of going back to Korea, but I was glad to be home for now.

My second phone call was to my wife, Joan, who was staying with her parents in Harvey, Louisiana. I told her that I was in San Francisco, heading to Herlong.

"I'll call you from there," I reassured her. "I know I can get my old job back."

Military Man

After I returned from Korea, I wanted to rejoin the army and become a career military man. However, I had two children and couldn't do that to my family. I thought of joining the army reserves, but it was too far away. The closest option was the California National Guard.

I was the only colored person in the Susanville unit, which made life more difficult. The others treated me much like the old days back in the South, calling me racist names, talking down to me, and treating me harshly. But just like in days past, that treatment didn't break my spirit; it only made me fight harder. Within six months, I recruited four more coloreds. Together, we held strong, enduring many racial slurs. Over time, the white guardsmen began to respect our hard work and dedication until we all worked as a collective unit with respect for each other.

Reinstatement

Caleb got his discharge a couple of months before me and was already working back at the depot. When I arrived in Herlong, I applied for temporary quarters. The staff recognized me, welcomed me back, and asked if I was ready to go back to work.

"Not yet," I responded. "Give me at least 10 days."

I called my wife with the good news, and she and our two children were back in Herlong four days later. These were days filled with happiness, gladness, and thankfulness to the all-powerful God. It was a time for rejoicing and being with my family. I spent the next few days living like Mr. Good Time Man—all play and no work. On the 12th day, I decided that it was time to get serious again. I stayed in temporary family quarters until the housing I applied for came through.

I asked Caleb if he had any trouble reinstating under his true name, and he said that, so far, he didn't have any trouble and easily corrected his file. This news made me feel comfortable enough to report for reinstatement under my true name. So, on Monday morning, March 15, 1953, Ardist Cooper, Jr., officially began employment at the Sierra Ordinance Depot in Herlong, California.

This is what my reinstatement document said:

Restoration after military service

Position Title: Fork Lift Operator, 1030a Service Series Grade

Salary: WB 5704-6, St. 3, $1.82 per hour

Organizational Designations: Ordinance, Miscellaneous Services Division, Labor & Vehicle Pool Branch

Headquarters: Sierra Ordinance Depot, Herlong, California, and Consummated March 30, 1953

Remarks: This action is subject to all applicable laws, ruling and regulations and may be subject to investigation and approval by this United States Civil Service Commission. This action may be corrected or canceled if not in accordance with all requirements. Served under Permanent Appointment under name Caleb [nmn] Cooper, D/B 2/9/27, Badge 12164, Separation Military Service 3/15/51. Name change from Caleb [nmn] Cooper correction to be made in employment records to Ardist Cooper, Jr.

Chapter 15

Justice

Adjusting to Civilian Life

I returned to civilian life facing many significant changes but, like the rest of my life, it was a challenging time. At only 20 years old, I was a Korean War veteran, a husband, and a father. I enjoyed coming home to my wife and two children and the renewed pleasure of managing my income and expenses. My new job as a forklift operator paid a little more and, even with the added expenses of my family, I immediately picked up my old plan to bring the rest of my Louisiana family out west. I felt as if my life wouldn't feel normal until that happened.

One of the disappointing adjustments was accepting that, no matter how I was treated in Korea, the people of Herlong still considered coloreds inferior to whites. In Korea, I felt equal to whites more than I ever had in my whole life. Mind you, it wasn't perfect, but it was the best I ever experienced.

Many colored folks fought the closed hearts in Herlong because we wanted to stick it to the white man and give him what he deserved. I know that doesn't sound very Christian, but it's the truth. We didn't feel that every white person was bad; we had plenty of white friends. We just wanted to stick it to the ones who kept pushing us down. Each time I won a fight against injustice, I felt that it wiped away a little bit of the wrongs done to my family and to me.

Challenging Authority

Big Cooper and Middle-size Cooper had observed a bar, seven miles away from the gate of the Sierra Ordinance Depot in Herlong, which served drinks and had a place to sit, talk, and drink. Although it was in California, the owner had set it up as an exclusive white tavern. Colored customers could buy liquor and stand outside at the window to drink it.

On my 21st birthday, my two brothers challenged this embarrassing and inhumane act by taking me for my first barstool encounter. When we sat down, the bartender told us that we weren't going to served us at the bar.

"Why?" I asked. "I have money."

The bartender, who was also the owner, said, "I don't serve coloreds inside."

After a few moments of looking around at the customers, including one woman who was sitting at the bar, we left the premises.

As I was leaving, I turned to the bartender and said, "Thanks for nothing."

We, the history-making brothers, filed a lawsuit in conservative Susanville, Lassen County, charging race discrimination. It was probably the first—and last—case of its kind. I am proud to say that we prevailed. We won all points, and received the maximum award allowed under the law, plus court costs, from an all-white judge and jury. I challenged society wherever I found a wrong that needed righting while staying active in church, working full time, and being with my young family.

By the end of 1953, we delivered another sibling to the Promised Land. When my sister Maiya and her husband, Mareck, both started jobs at the Sierra Ordinance Depot, I cautioned them to report to work on time and do their assignments exactly as told because there were no exceptions while on probation. Maiya and Mareck were new in town, but they soon learned how easy it was to settle in and find new friends. Herlong was small and you usually crossed paths with familiar faces at church, the local recreation center, the post office, or the movie theater.

Self-improvement

I registered to vote. I decided that I needed to learn how to change the things I could change and accept the things I couldn't. I focused on developing my skills because I believed in constant self-development. I always liked learning; I just hated school.

I was already active in the community, but I thought that, if I wanted to do more—to make more change—I needed to be a better communicator. At that time, I was a strong listener, knew how to work well with others, thought strategically, and figured out the steps needed to get something done. That was all good, but I also had weaknesses: I was a fourth-grade dropout, didn't own any real estate, and couldn't get my bank account above $300. I vowed to strengthen these weak points by enrolling in English and math night classes offered at the depot.

I drove down to the Veterans Administration building in Reno to see which courses I needed to become a California highway patrolman. This was "mission impossible" because you needed to be at least five feet, nine inches tall to qualify. (I was five feet, eight inches tall, if I stood on my tippy toes.) Nonetheless, becoming a highway patrolman was my goal, so I pressed on.

The VA gave me poor advice, saying that I needed to enroll in algebra, geometry, and English. I signed up, with the aid of the GI bill, for all three correspondence courses, and spent the next semester studying and taking the tests from home. I failed every test and dropped out of school for the second time.

Pressing Forward

Accepting that I would not be a California highway patrolman, I turned my efforts to my second goal: owning real estate. I went back to the VA to get a Certificate of Eligibility, which would help me buy a home; however, I didn't go through the process correctly. Every time I answered a request, I was required to fill out another form.

It didn't take long before I said, "Forget this mess. I'm tired of it." So I gave up the idea of becoming a homeowner and focused on something else.

I was good at coming up with ideas. Work had a suggestion box, asking employees for better and safer ways to do a job. If they accepted your suggestion, they paid you $50 for the idea. I submitted five or six suggestions and won the cash prize for safer pallet loading and unloading of boxcars and trucks. Oh, boy! That $50 felt like $500, and it helped boost my confidence again.

The correspondence courses were a failure, but I continued the night classes at the depot. Over the next several months, I took the Federal Service Entrance Exam to enter the Ordinance Supply Career Program. I applied and failed that entrance exam five times. I pressed on, applying for various in-house promotions, such as the crew lead man and foreman. I never got any of those promotions.

At that time, my goals were to make more money, own a piece of the rock, be an integral part of the administrative system, and feel better about myself. I hadn't achieved any of those goals no matter how hard and how often I tried. I started to wonder if I was capable of fulfilling my dreams.

While I felt heavy with self-doubt, I heard a voice inside saying, "Press forward!" and "Cross each bridge as you come to it."

This lifted my spirits enough to ignite my determination once again. I did not always struggle but, in that time, I focused on my goals and the fact that I wasn't achieving them. Looking back, that was a time filled with months of relaxation, happiness, and love. Sometimes, we spend so much time focusing on what we want that we forget to enjoy what we have along the way.

Boxing Dreams

I liked listening to boxing matches on the radio. They had a glamorous, exciting appeal. When I heard fights from Madison Square Garden, I followed the radio announcer intently. He described each blow so well that you could see in your mind what was happening in that boxing ring 3,000 miles away. Like children dreaming of growing up to be like their favorite baseball heroes, many professional and even more amateur boxers wanted to be like Joe Louis, the great "Brown Bomber," who was heavyweight champion of the world from 1937 to 1949.

I still remember several matches when Joe Louis was in his prime, fighting the other greats: light-heavyweight Billy Conn, nicknamed "The Pittsburgh Kid"; and Max Schmeling, a German boxer, who was heavyweight champion of the world from 1930 to 1932. When Joe came out the winner, those were happy days for me. I also followed Archie Moore, light-heavyweight world boxing champion from 1952 to 1959 and then again in 1961; and rough, tough middleweight Sugar Ray Robinson. You had to be tough to get past the other line of fighters who all wanted the championship.

Listening to these matches for so many years, I became interested in learning some boxing fundamentals. I trained seven days a week with a boxing coach, who taught me shadow boxing and other techniques. I learned a few punches and thought I developed a jab good enough to fight in a big match. Around that time, the 1956 Golden Gloves competition started in Las Vegas, Nevada. Thinking I was pretty good, I joined a group of amateurs and signed up with a trainer for the Reno boxing team.

We entered our names into the competition and drove to Las Vegas. We were all full of excitement all the way, but it was still a long, tiring trip. My fighting name was "Kid Cooper," middleweight. Once in Vegas, we were nervous and anxious to fight, so the waiting around made us feel like a cat scratching for dirt on a tin roof.

Up until my fight time, I kept visualizing myself as the Golden Gloves champion, even though we knew we weren't going to win any money. Strategically, we wanted to win because a win here let us fight in the Hollywood Bowl; then, a win there moved us into a match overseas. I wanted to win the "big three" so I could be a big-time professional, work my way up to fight some of the rated fighters, and get $300 for a four-round boxing match.

I won the Golden Gloves title that day! It was one of the most visceral and uplifting moments of my life. I was 24 years old and for the first time in my life, I truly felt as if I were somebody. Well, I felt like somebody for a few hours at least. Especially when the news reporters asked about my boxing plans. This type of attention was new to me, and all I could think of saying was that I looked forward to the Hollywood Bowl.

People told me that the Hollywood Bowl was a big match—big in importance and big in the crowd size. I didn't realize how big that crowd was until I saw them myself. To tell you the truth, there were so many people watching, they scared me. I was still a country boy used to small Louisiana farm towns and little Herlong. Seeing so many people packed into one place intimidated me so much, I couldn't loosen up enough to fight.

When my fight time came up, the walk from the dressing room into the ring seemed like three blocks. As everyone yelled and cheered, it frightened me so badly that I had trouble climbing into the boxing ring. I lost my very first match in the Hollywood Bowl.

I felt so depressed over my poor performance that, over 53 years later, I still kick myself about it. That night, I didn't return to the fighters' sleeping quarters. I left the stadium right after my fight and milled around the streets all night, feeling sorry for myself. For months, I punished myself mentally and emotionally, but eventually I went back to training for professional boxing.

Over the next few months, I booked some good boxing tickets, such as a four-round preliminary in Reno, Nevada; Boise and Callister, Idaho; Salt Lake City, Utah; Susanville, San Jose, and Oakland in northern California. I made a few dollars, but not enough to live on because, like most boxers, I was doing this on the side. I still had my full-time job at the depot and a family to support. Like the other part-time boxers, we continued boxing in hopes of winning a big purse.

I continued boxing for years and, when I later moved to San Francisco, I signed up with a new manager. With my community activities, family, and two jobs, I don't know how I managed to train two hours a day, seven days a week, but somehow I did. Then, after a couple of fights, my manager said that I couldn't make any money in this game unless I quit my jobs and trained full time. I needed to support my family, and still had big goals of owning a piece of the rock and moving the rest of my family out west, so I ended my boxing career.

Chapter 16

Pressing Forward

An NAACP Troublemaker

Over the next few months, I continued to press forward with my desire to right the world by fighting for equality and fairness at work and in the community. I also focused on my goals of owning land, bettering my education, and receiving promotions to higher-paying jobs.

By now, Herlong had its own NAACP (National Association for the Advancement of Colored People) chapter, which increased my determination and strength to fight for justice. I was proud to be a member because they reinforced the notion that I felt since I was a child: I was better than what other people told me I was, and I deserved more opportunities than I had received. To this day, I'm still a member.

We men and women who were serious about changing the world, vowed among ourselves to remain collectively bound and to remain loyal and active members of the most recognized civil rights organization in America. At work, this change started by making noise each time a white man passed me up for a promotion for which I was qualified, or if I heard of another colored

135

employee who didn't get a job he was qualified to receive. I also kept fighting against housing segregation, telling the authorities that their method of assigning family housing was a shame and disgraceful to humanity.

I notified the NAACP office and the authorities at the Sierra Ordinance Depot, informing them of their unfair labor practices. It didn't take long before management labeled me as a trouble-maker. Some people treated me coldly and did other little things to show that they were not pleased with my actions, but I pressed forward.

Making Changes

Southern folks always used sayings that I didn't fully understand until I became a grown man. One of them was, "If something's annoying you, and you can't do much about it, it's like having a fly in your buttermilk." Well, I was certainly a fly in the depot's buttermilk, but I didn't become a serious nuisance until they went too far with their housing discrimination.

The housing authority decided to remodel and repaint the inside of every housing unit. After many years, they still confined coloreds to the 200 block of the family units. During the remodeling, they moved families to the 300 and 400 blocks. In order to keep white and colored families segregated, they implemented a piggyback system. They first remodeled the 400 block, and then moved whites out of the 300 block to the newly remodeled units. Afterwards, they would remodel the old 300 block, and then move the coloreds from the old 200 block to the remodeled units. In other words, they were moving us from one segregated housing space to another.

Active NAACP members showed our displeasure by refusing the housing move when our turn came up. The housing authority asked a couple of times, and each time we politely refused. Then they threatened to deny us housing if we didn't move. While all this was going on, we informed the NAACP's local branch and regional office in San Francisco.

The corporate NAACP office in New York supported our fight and we had the support of the regional office's attorney, who once visited our branch and called Herlong the "Misplaced Mississippi." We also had assistance from the regional director, field secretary, some dynamic and well-known personalities, and the office's staff.

With the collective work of these men, women, and numerous volunteers, our Herlong chapter president led us through the circus of eliminating segregated housing on the depot. Through documented testimony, the Department of Housing in Washington, D.C., learned of our unfair practices and, seeing the severity of our situation, they sent army officers from Washington to conduct a full investigation.

The investigation took months to complete, but it was worth the wait. The Department of Housing announced that the Sierra Ordinance Depot's housing officer was guilty of housing discrimination, removed from his position, and temporarily replaced by a military captain while the depot conducted interviews over the next year. Washington ordered the new housing officer and the incoming administration to carry out the letter of the law in the spirit of fair housing, which meant absolutely no discrimination. *Another victory!* I felt elated.

Added to the sweet reward of this victory, they promoted a qualified colored person as the new senior housing officer—my brother, Caleb. After the Korean War, Caleb commuted to school at night and earned his bachelor's degree in business administration. Like me, he hoped for an opportunity and prepared himself to receive it.

Being prepared was always one of my unwritten rules to overcoming the setbacks in life. Preparing yourself doesn't always involve more school or training; sometimes, it's spiritual, physical, or mental. In the housing discrimination battle, I prepared myself spiritually and mentally to maintain the determination I needed to keep standing for what we collectively and individually believed during the nearly two-year battle. My family was growing, too. We had a third child on the way, and I had to prioritize my goals.

Restlessness Returns

By this time, you could say that, between work, community involvement, and my own playtime, my life was the most comfortable it had ever been. I kept busy in the community and stayed active in the First Baptist Church. No matter where I went, I couldn't walk down the street without passing several friends. It was my kind of hometown. Herlong still felt a little small, but I had enough recreation to keep myself entertained. I still enjoyed fishing and, during the season, hunted duck, cottontail rabbits, quail, pheasants, and deer. I could see the progress in the community as whites and coloreds interacted with each other more. It seemed as if significant changes were finally happening and there was no turning back.

But all that wasn't enough. I was coming into my sixth year working in Herlong when that familiar, inner longing was pulling me out of what was familiar and comfortable to go searching again. Unlike the other times, I knew where I was supposed to go and why I was going. This time, I was going to Hollywood to become a movie star.

I figured that I had the talent, and Hollywood was *hot* in those days. I was crazy enough to think that all I needed was to go down there, rub elbows with the movie stars, have someone discover me, and then become rich and famous. That was the extent of my plan, which was more planning than I ever did since running away from home.

I liked Los Angeles because it was a big city and we had a friend there named Mae, who used to live in Warden. She was like the mother from the South; even though she was a young girl, she knew just about everyone from Warden. Many moved to L.A. and, when they arrived, they would check in with her. Caleb and I used to go down and visit Mae at her house on Graham Avenue.

To help me save up for the big move, I signed up for an automatic payroll deduction plan to purchase a $50 Series E Savings Bond each pay period. That was the most advertised and popular way of saving and investing back then. You were encouraged to *Buy your savings bond today!* every time you opened the newspaper, listened to the radio, or watched TV.

Buying a $50 savings bond twice a month was a lot of money because I only made $75 a week back then; however, I was fueled by my desire to become a movie star in L.A., so we did what was necessary to make the move. I considered it part of my preparation. Since my desire to move was so strong, it made the extra $100 a month we lost to savings easier to bear. Some challenges tested my resolve a few times but, instead of taking me off track, these challenges kept me more focused than ever.

Challenging My Focus

While driving on the depot, I received one of these challenges when I got a speeding ticket. For violations on depot grounds, an army commissioner comes twice per week to hold court in place of a judge; however, you can request to have your case tried before a judge in Sacramento if you're willing to make the drive.

The depot's commissioner had a reputation. Whenever someone came before him, he'd just sock it to 'em! That worried me because things may have been friendlier between whites and colored, but they weren't *that* friendly. Truth be told, I was feeling ambitious back then, with two social victories under my belt. I thought I might have a chance to fight the ticket (even though I was speeding).

On my court date, the commissioner asked, "Mr. Cooper, do you want to be tried here or do you want to take your case to Sacramento?"

"I wouldn't mind takin' it to Sacramento, sir!"

The depot's commissioner ordered me to pay a cash bond of $50 before I could leave the hearing room, and then said they would notify me about my hearing date. About a week later, around 10 a.m., a U.S. federal marshal came up to me. I was busy at work, surrounded by co-workers, "Are you Ardist Cooper?"

"Yes, sir," I said. Right then, he handcuffed me. "Hey, I put up my $50! Why are you arrestin' me?"

"You're being arrested to go down for trial in Sacramento."

He pushed me into the squad car, which was a dirty, lowdown deal. Can you imagine the embarrassment and shame I felt from that scene? It was terrible. Those rascals decided to teach me a lesson, I guess. Maybe it was my history of fighting for civil rights or the fact that no one else ever chose to have their case tried in Sacramento; maybe it was a combination of both reasons. Whatever it was, the "powers that be" unfairly arrested me for the second time in my life.

On the way to Sacramento, you have to pass through Reno. The marshal took advantage of this trip to do a little gambling and locked me up in a Reno jail overnight while he had some fun. That night, a reporter came into the jailhouse looking for stories and asked why I was in there. I told him that I was on my way to Sacramento because of a speeding ticket.

"So you were in a stolen car?" he assumed.

"No, it was my car." I explained the whole story and, looking at the expressions on the reporter's face, I could tell that he didn't believe me.

If he could see how frightened I was, he could instantly see I was telling the truth. This was my second time in handcuffs and in a jail cell with many other people. That was dangerous because one of the many risks in prison is that what goes on behind prison walls is a secret. If the police wanted to have a little fun and let the inmates rough me up, they'd turn a blind eye and I could do nothing to protect myself.

The marshal took his sweet time in Reno, even though he was aware of the trial schedule. We arrived in Sacramento the next day too late for my hearing, so I had to spend another night in jail. When I finally stood before the judge, the records showed that I had $50 on the books. The defense attorney turned to the judge, "Your Honor, I don't know why this man is here. He's got his bail paid in full."

The cotton pickin' crooked judge knew this and didn't care. He ignored the attorney, looked down at me and asked, "How much do you think I should charge you?"

"Well, nothin', Your Honor. I been in jail for two days!"

The judge slammed down his gavel and said, "$10 charge. Bailiff, see that Mr. Cooper receives the other $40 in the mail. Case dismissed."

Well, they sure got me. They humiliated me at work and scared me half to death while I was in jail. I lost two days' work, they added to my unjust prison record, and I spent two nights in jail. To top it off, those kind folks charged me nearly a day's pay for all of their fun.

After that episode, I focused on getting myself back on track. Losing all of that time and money made me more determined to save and move to L.A. Then, another challenge hit.

One Friday evening after work, I drove to my favorite fishing hole to relax and do a little fishing. At nightfall, I packed up to leave, but my car wouldn't start. No matter how I fussed with it, nothing worked, and I stayed on the creek bank all night long. To make matters worse, I didn't even catch any fish that day. Early the next morning, a friend also came to fish. He helped me get the car running and I thought that was all good.

Then one morning, I came out of my home to find all four car tires slashed. I complained to the police, telling them about this obvious act of vandalism. I suspected that it was due to an act of retribution for a skirmish I caused with my foreman and superintendent when they passed me up for promotion again. They gave the job to someone less experienced, newer, and white. I filed a grievance, demanding a formal hearing. I told the fine law people at the depot that it wasn't a coincidence that someone had slashed my tires the day after I filed the grievance. The police dismissed me, "Yeah, yeah, yeah. Did you *see* anybody?"

I thought, "No, of course I didn't see anybody. If I did, I wouldn't be comin' to you now, would I?"

They sent me out the door, refusing to file a report or investigate. Someone wanted to punish me for making fuss about the injustice in that depot. Slashing my tires was serious punishment because I didn't have money to replace them. For the next few months, my family and I walked everywhere or caught rides with friends. It took a long time to save enough money to replace one tire at a time.

Yes, that was punishment for us. I'm sure the vandals and unfair administration hoped that their acts would slow me down and weaken my resolve; instead, these acts made me really want to go after them more aggressively to get even.

The Water Fountain

While waiting for the grievance hearing, I had another run-in with the senior staff. I worked in a warehouse connected to an office building where 10 women and one man worked—all white, of course. An army major sat in an office looking out into the administrative area. The warehouse didn't have a drinking fountain, so it was customary for us workers to use the drinking fountain in the office. To reach the fountain, we had to walk past all of the desks. We'd walk past the office workers without interrupting them, take our quick drink, and get right back to work.

I was doing just that one day when the major marched out of his office, snatched the hat off my head, and shouted at me, "Don't you *ever* come in this office again with your hat on! Don't you know that it's a disgrace to these women?"

After all the years in the South, I knew what he meant by "these women"—he meant "these *white* women." He was a southerner, and southern men are very careful about coloreds acting respectfully around their women. His action was racially motivated, but my military training helped me remain low key.

I swallowed my anger and quietly said, "Yes, sir."

I reached for my hat and walked out without taking a drink. The major had never shown any resentment to me before, or said anything during the numerous other times I passed by to get a drink. However, this time, he felt some reason to come out and give me a hard time. This may not sound like a big deal in these modern times, but it was a deeply humiliating experience for me that day.

Can you imagine the embarrassment I felt as a grown man to have the major come out and scold me in front of everyone as though I were a child? Being a colored man scolded in front of whites made it even worse. Then, having him physically pull my hat off my head was way out of line. In fact, it was so out of line that, before the day ended, three of the office women and the man came to me saying they thought the major's act was malicious and, if I went to the personnel office to file charges, they would be witnesses for me.

The next day, I reported the incident to the head of personnel. She was a high-ranking civilian woman, who had been there for many years, but she tried to dismiss the incident, "Well, don't worry about it. I'm sure the major was just having a bad day."

I told her that the other office workers thought he behaved maliciously, but she continued waving me away. She didn't want to bring attention to the office. If she filed a complaint, it would go to the commanding officer, who was a colonel. Then there could be a formal hearing. If the colonel found that the major acted out of line, the colonel could have the major court-marshaled or transferred. The colonel could have done anything, but he needed to see the complaint first, and that's what the personnel officer wanted to hide.

When I kept pressing, she offered to write the major a letter of reprimand and send me a copy. I never received a copy and concluded that she never intended to write it and would sweep the whole matter under the table.

The next morning, the office workers, who offered to be my witnesses, asked, "Well, did you file charges?"

I told them I tried but the head of personnel refused to file a report. They were surprised and urged me to keep fighting, suggesting other methods to report him, but I decided not to pursue them.

I never went in to get a drink of water again. The white men still walked from the warehouse with their hat on and never had a problem but, even with my hat off, I wanted to stay clear of the major's path. That position rotated every two years or so, and I think he had another six months before he rotated out. So long as he was there, I made sure that I never had contact with him again.

That experience renewed my old thought, "This job is dead end and I need to find a better place."

Like all those times since I ran away from the farm, the strong urge welled up inside me to move on and find a place that offered me what I deserved. I was better than what they believed and I wanted to prove it.

The Tractor and the Pole

Months before, I had filed a grievance with personnel because of a denial for an opportunity to compete. The hearing date finally arrived to discuss my grievance and, this time, I was victorious! Without much resentment, the committee gave me another job opportunity. They offered to let me compete for a small lots supervisor position and trained me with the other people competing for the job.

I spent three weeks in training and, in my opinion, completed it with honors. I always followed instructions well and learned by watching. This time, I did all that and took notes because I wanted to make sure I got everything right.

The personnel office took their sweet time scheduling final evaluations for us trainees. During this time, my guardian angel once again decided that it was time to move on. As in my previous experiences, this push came in an unorthodox manner.

At the end of a work shift, the forklift and tractor drivers gathered at the checkout office 10 minutes before checkout time. I wanted to run an errand nearby before going home, so I borrowed a co-worker's tractor. On my way back, the accelerator jammed, causing me to go faster than I wanted. Without thinking, I looked down to see what might be causing the problem.

With my head down, I couldn't see that I was heading towards the telephone pole. I glanced up in time to see it right before I hit it straight on. The impact broke the pole and the tractor's steering rod. Total damage: around $300. The investigators couldn't tell if the steering rod broke before or after the accident.

When questioned, I said, "I plead guilty of not havin' official permission for this trip."

The accident report stated that "no lives were endangered or lost," and a typical punishment would be that I would pay for the damages to the tractor and telephone pole. On the extreme end, punishment could be 30 days' suspension without pay.

This was how the administrators removed troublemakers. Since they called me a troublemaker on numerous occasions, the administrators decided to fire me. They claimed that my little insubordinate accident was reason enough to fire a 10-year career civil service employee with a strong work record and veteran's preference.

That little accident changed the course of my life. I was out of the running for the supervisor position as well as losing a 10-year career. No more waiting and saving, no more excuses. The door of opportunity opened wide for this runaway child, a fourth-grade dropout student, nurtured by the spirit of God. I was willing to strive honestly for excellence. I needed to move my family out of Herlong immediately.

From the time of the tractor accident to the agency firing me 60 days later, I decided that I would travel to a new area with my wife, sons, and daughter. I had the full support of my family, which was a great comfort to me.

We all said, "Here we go!"

Chapter 17

City Life

Rags to Riches

In my 10 years at Herlong, I achieved several goals. My most important achievements were the number of family members I helped free from the South. After I returned from Korea, another sister joined our family in Herlong and my mom visited for a while, but she didn't want to stay.

I realize now that I had a selfish, narrow view of the whole situation. I thought that, because I lived in Herlong, then it must be the Promised Land. I thought that Herlong was the place I must move my entire family so we could all be together. In my selfishness and blind desire to free them, I didn't accept the fact that Herlong may not have been comfortable for everyone, and that some may have wanted to move elsewhere.

I didn't have the sense to see that if my goal was to free them from the South so they could live a rags-to-riches story, then anywhere they could find a better life should do. Since I was still blind to that realization, I kept pulling my family to come to me. When they didn't stay or they didn't want to come, I somehow felt as if I failed in my goal. My pride got in the way.

Renting in the City

After my abrupt dismissal from Sierra Ordinance Depot, it dawned on me to call the NAACP for representation. I wanted them to help me appeal the dismissal action against me. The NAACP region office accepted my request and handled my case out of San Francisco. They knew it would take a while and hundreds of meetings. For efficiency, they told me to move my family there. I never liked the big city, but Joan was eager to move out of Herlong's small town and small-minded ways.

I agreed, thinking that it was a temporary move. Although I wanted something better, and knew that Herlong was a dead end, I still had the prideful mindset of a young man. I fought the depot to win my old job back and show that they did me wrong. I wanted justice.

Throughout this time, I was blind to the fact that my move was predestined and, as in all of my other moves, the will of God. I didn't recognize my guardian angel's hand at that tugging feeling to move on; I just blamed it on a young man's restlessness.

It wasn't easy settling into San Francisco because I couldn't secure a job, even with a civil service job record and veteran's status. Joan found employment at a guesthouse to help feed the family while I stayed home, caring for the children. Another difficulty was that coloreds and whites lived in segregated neighborhoods, and whites confined coloreds to a small area of the city.

Even though the population was getting bigger, our area wasn't growing much. We looked in the paper for rental units, and asked other colored folks from the NAACP or the store about available rentals or areas where we should look. It took many searches before we found a place to live—partly because there were so few vacancies and partly because most people didn't want small children on their property.

At first, our new home was good because the landlady lived next door and didn't mind having children around. Joan had someone to talk to and get advice about where to get groceries or other things nearby. A few months later, the landlady decided that having renters with small children was too much trouble, and she ordered us out.

Buying our House

It took so long to find a rental that I didn't want to go through the process again just to face eviction a few months or a year later for some reason or another. I decided that it was time to buy our own house.

For the down payment, I used the money we saved for our intended move to L.A. and applied for a veteran homeowner's loan. Even with this down payment and favorable financing, we still had trouble because I wasn't working, Joan wasn't making much, and we were colored. We didn't know any colored realtors and very few white realtors would represent us. However, we eventually found a realtor who knew the colored neighborhoods well. At first, I was excited about owning a piece of the rock, but my excitement soon turned into disgust.

We looked at house after house and, as soon as the owners or other realtors saw that colored folks wanted to buy the house, they suddenly said that they sold it. I got so fed up that I told Joan I didn't want to look at another house and didn't care if we all lived on the street after that.

Thankfully, Joan kept looking until she finally found an owner who would sell to us. The Lord blessed me with a patient woman and a house on Victoria Street. It was a "junior five," with two bedrooms, one full bath, a kitchen, a dining room, and a one-car attached garage. At a cost of $15,500, our monthly payments were $94 including tax and insurance. We were moving on up! Nearly 60 years later, we still live in that same house.

The Long Fight

As soon as my family moved to San Francisco, the NAACP and I began fighting the case against Sierra Ordinance Depot. For many long months, the depot cited government regulation after government regulation, and personnel rule after rule; the NAACP's attorneys cited law after law in reply. After several months and many hours, the depot gave their final word: Guilty as charged.

We appealed the case, moving it up to the chief of ordinance in Sacramento. They questioned the solidity of our appeal, and then agreed that the depot handled me fairly. After that, we appealed the case to the Washington Civil Service Commission. Less than 45 days later, we received a copy of a letter they sent to the Sierra Ordinance Depot, telling the depot that the maximum penalty they could legally charge was having me pay for the damages incurred and 30 days without pay.

This letter gave the NAACP team (and me) a great deal of hope. We were confident of our victory. More correspondences passed back and forth for another 16 months. Then, we received the victorious decision nullifying the actions made by the Sierra Ordinance Depot 21 months prior, and they retroactively restored me back to my employment. This was a shouting historical victory—the first of its kind at the depot.

My soul danced with joy, singing, "Justice at last ... justice at last!"

After the Sierra Ordinance Depot received orders to reinstate me, I applied for my old job and soon got word to start work again. Joan didn't want to leave the bright lights of the city or our new home, and we agreed that the children were better off in a larger town than Herlong. For the next six months, I worked in Herlong and drove back to San Francisco on the weekends. If I thought I had little money before, I had even less now because I had to support two households. Honestly, though, I didn't mind it. Mentally, physically, and spiritually, I was rejoicing from my victory in winning my job back.

Every family in Herlong knew about the historical victory, but very few employees talked to me about it.

"So what?" they said. "The NAACP got his job back."

The NAACP Herlong branch didn't use the victory as a fundraiser or membership drive and kept the event low key. As soon as I settled back in, I got involved with church and community activities again, reacquainted myself with old friends, and enjoyed the satisfaction of working every day. I enjoyed myself so much that I really didn't have any serious intentions of moving back to San Francisco full time, although part of me knew that I must consolidate my family soon.

San Francisco Cabbie

Life moved along smoothly in my familiar Herlong routine. Then one day, without any forethought, I threw a few household items into my 1956 white Lincoln and drove home to my wife and children. It was another one of those moments where I just felt a strong need to take action. After so many years of treating Herlong as my home, I knew it was time to welcome Victoria Street.

I sealed the decision by sending a resignation letter to the personnel office. Herlong had its challenges, but leaving was very difficult. I arrived there a boy—at 14 years, nine months, and two days old. Then I became a man there. In Herlong, I met my wife and we started a family. All of my brothers and sisters who moved out west lived in Herlong or in nearby Reno. Most of my friends and acquaintances lived in that sagebrush patch in the desert. I had many bad times and many good times and, for all of my struggles, Herlong was home.

I was still a country boy who enjoyed wide, open spaces. It took at least three months before I stopped fighting the hills of San Francisco and accepted it as my new home. San Francisco became my adopted earthly place of abode until the Lord Jesus Christ comes back to take me with him.

I immediately became active in the local NAACP branch and found time to volunteer many hours in the downtown regional office on Market Street. After work, at least three or four days a week, I walked to the colored neighborhoods, going door to door, telling them about the NAACP, and asking them to be members. I became acquainted with some hard-working men and women, who were fighting for freedom to make this world a better place, fueled by faith and hope for the day when men and women of all colors would walk together in harmony. Many didn't live to see it become a reality, but I testify that their hopes became truth.

Within a few short months, I found my first full-time work in my newly adopted city. At that time, Yellow Cab was the largest cab company in the Bay Area. Under long-time pressure by the NAACP, Yellow Cab finally agreed to hire colored drivers once they reached 25 years of age. As soon as I became that age, I went down to their Turk Street office and applied. I think they had one or two colored drivers in 1957, but the big push for more happened in 1958 when I started, so there weren't enough of us yet to get society accustomed to colored drivers.

Just because Yellow Cab said it was all right to have colored drivers, it didn't mean that the passengers thought so too. Many times, people started to get into the cab, saw me, and backed out saying that they had changed their mind or they'd catch the next cab. Other times, I'd get a radio order to pick up a fare so I'd run up the steps to the house and ring the bell.

When the person saw me (if they were polite), they'd say, "Oh, I don't want a cab," and quickly shut the door.

If they weren't polite, they'd tell me what they were really thinking. I'd go back to the car and radio the dispatcher, saying that the passenger didn't want a cab. That type of rejection hurt and I told the dispatcher how I felt.

"You know they didn't want me because I'm black."

The dispatcher would sound offended and say that they wouldn't send them another cab, but I know they always did. Business is business.

After some time, people slowly got used to coloreds driving Yellow Cabs. We had to be very respectable and follow the strict rules of being nice, remembering that the customer was always right and that we drivers had no rights. They meant every word of it. I was very respectable because I didn't want to lose my job. Their strict rules were easy to bear because I liked driving a cab so much.

By driving, I learned and experienced things that I wouldn't be able to do or see otherwise. I always enjoyed learning new skills and knowledge, and I quickly learned how to get to the many hospitals, restaurants, hotels, and airports, but it took nearly six months before I felt comfortable in truly knowing where to go and how to move easily from point to point. As in my other jobs, I mastered cab driving through determination and a goal for excellence.

I drove the swing shift five days a week for eight hours a day. The first few days, driving around the up-and-down city, with its maze of congested streets, frustrated me so much that I wanted to quit. I did not like the hills and had trouble figuring my way around. However, the $4 to $5 that I earned in tips each night—big money in those days—kept me going. By the grace of God, I survived driving a cab as I learned my way around the city, taking radio orders, finding addresses, and delivering passengers to their destinations. It was definitely a new adventure and a challenge for me.

In my era of working for Yellow Cab, they considered drivers professional community servants. We reported for work in a dark suit or uniform and black shoes. If someone called for a pickup, we didn't go blowin' no horn, waiting for someone to come out. We got our fanny out, knocked on their door, and, if it was a lady, escorted her to the cab. We always opened the cab door for women who were getting in and out. When we dropped them off, we waited for them to enter the building before driving off. Cab inspectors circulated in every shift, making sure we stuck with their strict policies.

Back then, we needed clearance from the police department to show we were trustworthy. Yellow Cab also spot-checked us for honesty by sending people into our cabs, pretending to be drunk and waving money in our faces. These decoys would also ask about ladies of the night, just to see if the drivers were pimping.

Two Priests

For a big city, San Francisco was less open-minded about equality than neighboring towns, such as Oakland. I later learned that it was because many of the rich people in San Francisco had roots in the South and were holding tightly to the old southern ways. They owned big businesses and ran them with the same closed, southern mind. When people see that attitude at work, they bring it home. As a result, San Francisco stayed closed-minded until the 1960s.

San Francisco is a busy but small city—about seven miles long by seven miles wide. As small as it is, I drove between 80 to 100 miles each shift. The city was growing so fast with new construction that, when I passed through an area again, I'd wonder when they tore down a building or put up one on a corner. I had to stay sharp, always observing and remembering.

I became very skilled at driving through the many intersections and weaving through traffic, and had an accident-free record for the first four and one-half years. Then, one early evening, I was at the intersection of Pine Street and Presidio Avenue at the wrong time. I learned that they time the streetlights on Pine Street in sequence so, when you hit one green light, you can usually get them all if there isn't any traffic. I was driving smoothly along Pine Street with a female passenger heading towards UCSF Hospital. Then, from the corner of my eye, I saw a car with two priests in it coming at me through the intersection. I slammed on my brakes in time to lessen the impact, but we still hit each other.

Thankfully, no one was hurt, but I was upset because of my ruined driving record. When the police came, I told them that the priest ran the red light and my passenger said the same thing. She was white, so I thought for sure that the police would believe us.

I didn't want to argue against a priest, so I added, "Whatever the priests say, I'm not gonna make no fuss."

Naturally, the priests said that they had a green light and the accident was my fault.

The accident didn't damage my car, so I continued driving the rest of my shift. Later, I checked the cab into the dispatcher and gave written notice of the accident. They told me to report to the front office the next morning, and reminded me of the company policy: When an accident occurs at an intersection, you got a minimum of two days off without pay. Yellow Cab believes that accidents don't happen unless you're there, and accidents only happen at intersections when two idiots meet.

The next morning, I reported to the office, and the interviewing manager pulled up my long driving record. He was impressed and said that it was a shame the accident had to happen. He told me the police believed that the priests ran the red light, then he asked, "Who's going to tell two priests that they're not telling the truth?"

"I'm not," I answered.

The manager had to follow policy by reading me the company rules about accidents occurring at intersections. He said that Yellow Cab would pay for the auto damages and any other claims that came up. He wanted to be lenient by giving me only one day off without pay, but he said that I was out of the running for the gold watch, which drivers got when they drove five years without an accident.

All I could say was, "Well, so close yet miles from the finish line."

This reminded me of a saying we often used in the army, which said, "You only get points for closeness when you are dropping bombs or throwing hand grenades."

My Second Job

For the first two years driving a cab on the swing shift, I hustled to pick up as many passengers as I could and put all of my tips towards the household income. I saw many possibly rewarding opportunities, which I couldn't take advantage of because I didn't have any extra money. Then, a green light flashed in my mind: I'm only working eight hours a day and I'm doing that at night, which meant that I had time to get another full-time job during the day.

I was used to hard work and I had goals. I still had family to bring out west and I wanted to increase my money stack. Thinking that my civil service status gave me an advantage, I applied at the post office for a mail-carrier position. They weren't interested in reinstating anyone because in their abstract way of thinking, they worried that if you didn't perform according to their rules, they'd have a tough time firing you.

My next stop was the Public Health Service Hospital on 15th Avenue and Lake Street. Back in 1958, I applied for a work transfer from the Sierra Ordinance Depot to this hospital but they weren't hiring at that time. This time, they accepted me the same day I applied. I made $1.77 an hour, working 8 a.m. to 4:30 p.m. with Tuesdays and Wednesdays off. This worked well for me because I drove a cab from 5:30 p.m. to 1:30 a.m. and had Sundays and Mondays off. The hospital assigned me to work as a dietary worker, which meant that we worked in the kitchen preparing and delivering food trays to the patients.

For the next 15 years, I continued working two full-time jobs and volunteering serious hours at the NAACP and in church activities. I chose a tiring lifestyle because I thought I was going to make the world a better place. I deceived myself into thinking that, if I continued working hard and volunteering, my commitment would accomplish all of my goals. I stayed focused, believing that, on a scale of 1 to 5, I held a 4.0 average in productivity.

Chapter 18

Social Revolution

A Worthwhile Donation

When you drive a cab, you hear many truths and untruths and meet some interesting people. One of the most interesting conversations was with a white male passenger. I don't know how the conversation started, but he told me that he had just visited his wife in the hospital and she needed a blood transfusion. Each pint of blood cost $25, so he asked his many acquaintances, who he considered friends, but none of them would step forward to donate. Listening to his story, I decided that he needed a helping hand.

I told him that I would donate a pint of blood at a nearby blood bank, and I'd announce his need at the church where I was an active member. All he had to do was tell me his name, his wife's name, and the hospital to send the blood. I kept my word and, although I don't know how many church members donated, I am satisfied that enough was donated to meet his need.

For all the months since he first got into my cab, I drove the same cab on the evening line at the St. Francis Hotel on Powell Street.

Then, one evening about a year later, the man and his wife came up to the cab asking, "Is your name Ardist Cooper?"

All I could get out was yes before the man exploded with joy, saying how he met me a year ago when he shared his story about his wife's need for blood donations. After she was well again, the man and his wife spent months asking cabbies their name. It was a joy for them to thank me personally. It was joy for me to see his wife on her feet!

After that, they sent many cards inviting Joan and me over to their house for dinner. We never joined them, although we appreciated their kind offers. We knew it wouldn't be wise to accept because they lived in a white neighborhood, and we would just be asking for trouble. We never explained that to them because they may have argued or been embarrassed. We just continued to decline their invitations politely. They exchanged Christmas cards with us for the next several years and, like many happenings in life, we eventually lost touch.

Haight–Ashbury

While driving a cab in San Francisco, I was able to see firsthand how a group of less than 100 white kids—even if you counted their cats and dogs—started a worldwide revolution. They first lived in the Upper Grant area between Vallejo and Broadway. When the system figured out a way to kick them out of that area, they relocated to the Haight–Ashbury district.

The existing Haight–Ashbury residents called them "beatniks" and didn't like them. Broadway was a popular tourist area full of nightlife. The residents were skittish of the rebellious and unwashed look of the beatniks, and decided they were bad for business. After a short time, the news media gave them the names "hippies" and "flower children," and that's when they grew like flowers.

Haight–Ashbury grew from 100 people to over 200,000 in no time. Thousands—young, old, rich, poor, and all ethnic groups— came from all over the country and the world, to see this social revolution. The flower children broke rules; blocked streets with their crowds; and dressed, behaved, and talked in ways completely opposite of the practices of our time—from conservative and moderate to oblique. I'm not sure what they were fighting for, and I don't think they really knew either, but they knew that they wanted something different from the rigid ways around them.

In those days, you almost had to put on a suit and tie just to go to a hamburger joint. Men and women couldn't go outside without a hat on, and women always wore gloves and looked very presentable, as if they were going to church. So, it was shocking, scandalous, and exciting to see these white children doing unexpected things, like pulling off their shoes and shirts, sitting around on the streets, and walking around unwashed. They dressed in unusual ways with ragged jeans and torn shirts.

It didn't take long before the flower children became a sideshow for tourists and made Haight–Ashbury the hottest spot in town. Tourists would come in on an airplane from all over the world, ask me to drop them off at the Fairmont Hotel, and tell me to wait while they changed their clothes. If they were staying at the Fairmont you knew they had money but, a few minutes later, they'd come down in their flower children or hippie clothes, wearing some kind of perfume that made them smell like they hadn't taken a bath in days. Yes, someone made perfume to smell like hippies and people were buying it!

Carrying their cameras and dressed in their costumes, the passengers would say, "Take us to Haight–Ashbury!"

As I drove my passengers through those streets, it was like watching a TV show. The tourists seemed excited and scared at the same time. Once they saw the hippies, my passengers would shake their heads and talk in dismayed amazement. Most were too scared to get out of the car and walk around. I didn't blame them. This new and radical sight turned their world upside down.

They'd just look out of the cab window repeating, "I don't believe it!"

I wouldn't have believed it either had I not seen it so many times. Being in it every day, I adjusted to it incrementally, but those tourists were in shock—especially the ones who knew that their children were probably somewhere in that crowd.

As I was driving through those streets, I thought of the Winnie the Pooh story where Pooh and his friends were looking and searching for a long time. When one thought to ask what they were looking for, the other friend replied that he didn't know. Then another friend wondered how they were going to know when they found it.

Watching this Haight–Ashbury revolution, I too wondered how they were going to know that they found "it" when they didn't know what they were looking for. Looking at their faces and the way they moved—lackadaisical and lost—the flower children seemed as if they were on a never-ending search.

They destroyed moral family principles and broke many care-givers and parents' hearts as they rejected years of loving care. Up until that time, families had done a lot of nurturing so their children would be wholesome and respectable. We were teaching what society had set up as being good and right: be neat and dressed when you went out; be clean and orderly; go to school and get your degree. Then, these children just dropped out of school and society by the thousands.

While driving my cab, I met many parents who cried real tears, with sadness covering their brow, saying things like, "Where did I go wrong?" and "I don't know what happened to those children!"

I asked these parents, "If it all could be rewound, what could we have done?"

Naturally, we knew the answer: "Nothing."

I believe that society had been quietly restless for a long time, and generation after generation were sowing the seeds. The flower children, who came up from those seeds, spread the restlessness and the need for change to the minds they touched. Yes, this movement affected our nation and spread throughout the world, but not everyone thought the flower children were bad. A lot of us, like me, thought that they were a good thing because their rebellious ways broke it all down. We didn't have to walk around dressed up all the time, which was a good thing.

The flower children also broke down many racial barriers. People started to look at coloreds as human beings—even in old-time San Francisco. The flower children drew in hundreds of thousands of different types of people, which caused society to wake up and accept all people as members of planet Earth created by God. Mind you, that whole time was a fiasco, but they did uplift tolerance. As in the many battles for social change before this, worthwhile progress doesn't come like a neatly wrapped package on Christmas morning.

The Revolution's Dark Side

Aggressive movements come with some good and some bad. At first, the drug LSD filtered through only a little. The young people gathered in Haight–Ashbury just to hang out and enjoy their new lifestyle called "free love." Many children didn't have to work because they came from rich parents who didn't want them back home, shaming them. These parents paid their children's rent and gave them plenty of money to eat and live. Later, rebels moved into Haight–Ashbury, bringing their drugs and trouble, which was when things started to get nasty.

I counseled poor blacks who rode in my cab, saying, "Look man, you guys are out here with these white folks. When they go inside and decide to take a bath, they got somewhere to go. What's gonna happen to you? You ain't got *nowhere* to go."

Some blacks with money and an education were also out there with the flower children, such as a professor from San Francisco State College whom I knew at Herlong when he taught at Lassen County College. He was the only black person teaching up there, and then he moved to San Francisco and got a job at State. Now *he* had somewhere to go, but most of the other blacks didn't. They just wanted to hang out.

Hippies from Europe, Asia, and all over America flooded Haight–Ashbury until they spilled out into other parts of the city. All day, the hippies ate, slept, and "made *loooove*, honey!" They panhandled at Golden Gate Park until that whole area became dangerous. Of course, in any group, some decide to be slummy, and they ruin everything. After a while, the city forbade them to hang out and cleaned up the area. Then the drugs came in and the hippies stayed high all day.

The NAACP had many marches and protests in those days, especially in the 1960s. Some joined for the glamour, I guess, and wanted to be on TV and brag about what they did. These people just wanted to be rowdy for attention, so we couldn't use them because they could get us all arrested. That would put us out of business too fast and we knew we had to abide by the law, no matter what we were doing. Our focus was to challenge the law on its terms; however, the hippies weren't that organized. They allowed anyone to join, even those who joined to cause trouble.

I didn't realize how much pressure blacks felt until the hippie movement relieved some of it from us. The trouble was that, while we felt pressure from one end, it put more pressure on the other end. While minorities were getting more rights, society's moral values declined. Wiser people could see that and warned us about the fall, but I couldn't see it back then as I do now. The foolish time had come and we couldn't do anything about it.

I believe that what's supposed to happen will happen because this world is always revolving. From my teachings, I learned that nothing under the sun is new. Ecclesiastes 1:9 says, "The thing that hath been, it is that which shall be; and that which is done is that which shall be done: and there is no new thing under the sun."

What ignited the flower-child movement happened at some point in history and continued to brew for some time, even though we couldn't see it. The civil rights fighting from the late 1940s somewhat smoothed the way for those who felt that there had to be a change. Then, all of a sudden, the white people who held the reigns against change decided that they were tired of the way it was and created that change. It was like a new day.

Looking back, we can compare the 1960s with the wild 1920s. I think many necessary changes were birthed out of the liberal movements from the '60s to the '70s. Where young and old protested collectively for serious issues to be heard, such as voting rights, jobs, school, and housing.

Chapter 19

Forward and Backward

Still a Troublemaker

My day job at the Public Health Service Hospital felt like Herlong all over again. The administrative staff and supervisors were white, and coloreds could only work in the back of the kitchen, washing dishes and serving food. I soon learned that the hospital only gave coloreds what I call menial, hard-labor jobs.

After preparing the patients' meals, we'd load up the food on carts, rushing to deliver all of the meals on time. The hospital wanted us to serve each patient, so we had to ladle the food in each bowl or serve it on the plate. One person served about 30 patients, and their food was supposed to arrive hot, but the time-consuming task of serving each patient made that very difficult. Then, we rushed to clean our cart, pick up the patients' trays, and wash dishes. They had us working, working, working nonstop at that crazy pace for eight hours straight, every day.

I was new at this job, but the others had done it for years. I never worked with so many women before and boy, they could be cruel! When I complained, they told me that, if I couldn't handle the heat, I should get out of the kitchen. The women were used to putting up with anything.

The men asked them, "Why are you doing all this?"

They'd say, "Well, we got a job."

We men talked about our work conditions, saying, "Man, this is *murder*! Let's try to talk to the head dietician about this because we need more people serving."

It was almost impossible to deliver all the food trays in time without causing an accident. I told the administrators that we needed to add a few more people per shift and would still have plenty of work to keep us moving fast, but they were similar to the people in Herlong regarding their attitudes, supervisor–worker relationships, and short-sighted choices for promotion.Of course, the supervisor wouldn't listen. He said if we didn't like the job, then we should quit. Just like back in Herlong, they were unconcerned about the employees' working conditions. The hospital didn't know I was still a troublemaker, looking for justice.

On Sept. 7, 1960, I sent a letter to a judge in the House of Representatives, citing the unjust firing of government employees. Then, on November 24, 1960, I sent a letter to a congressman, telling him that we were overworked and that the supervisors wouldn't meet with us to discuss our problems. This started the ball rolling. The congressman sent a letter to the head dietician in Washington, D.C., which surprised everyone because no one had ever complained about work conditions.

After investigations, my complaint resulted in a change of policy where one person served only 15 patients instead of 30. We still hustled, but it was a lot more manageable. A few months later, they gave us new carts designed to hold prepared food trays. This let us prepare trays in the kitchen, which made it a lot easier to serve everyone on time and keep their food hot.

Another advance from our complaint was that the Public Health Service Hospital instituted a new policy allowing two 10-minute breaks every eight-hour shift, such as one break in the morning and one in the evening or late afternoon. This was similar to how it was on the farm where you would get water in the morning and then again in the evening. Before this, breaks on jobs didn't exist.

I never had a break in Herlong or as an extra gang worker for the railroad. Before the new policy, I never thought about breaks at all.

When someone came up to me in the past, complaining that he needed a break, I'd say, "What are you talkin' about? You got a break when you got the job!"

When the hospital hired me, government agencies were considering but had not yet implemented employee breaks. I believe that our complaint helped move that issue along so that all civil service employees received breaks. Then, once the civil service jobs started that policy, other companies followed.

Pushing Forward

I stayed in the food service position for 10 months, and then took a position in the labor/gardening area for 11 months. I always strove for other hospital positions that were more challenging and paid more. The engineering superintendent managed gardeners as well as plumbers, carpenters, electricians, and painters.

When I heard that the apprentice carpenter retired, I applied for his position. During the interview, the superintendent said that the apprentice carpenter stayed in that position for 17 years without a promotion, and no colored person ever worked in the carpentry shop. He gave me fair warning about what to expect, and then admitted that the only reason why the other guy was an apprentice for 17 years was that he didn't show any initiative.

The superintendent decided to assign me as labor for six months. My job was to sweep the shop, load and unload material, and assist the three carpenters. If I proved myself and showed initiative during those six months, he'd hire me as an apprentice carpenter.

I was ambitious back then. I accepted the opportunity, knowing that it would be a piece of cake. At first, I wasn't interested in the carpentry work, but the scornful looks I received from the carpenters and the degrading way they talked to me energized me to learn more and become a skilled carpenter. I vowed that I would master carpentry. The others gave me very little direction and tried not to teach me anything, but I used my trusted skills of observation to learn how they worked and watch their techniques.

Sometimes the carpenters stood around talking, saying "nigger this" and "nigger that," knowing that I could hear them. I never said a thing to them because I knew that it would keep me from getting the apprentice carpenter job.

They tried to antagonize me by saying, "This floor is dirty!" Even though the floor was clean, I wouldn't argue. I'd grab the broom in a hurry and start sweeping. It didn't take long to learn the types of lumber used in the shop and their various dimensions. Carpenters requested the material by name, hoping to trip me up, but I always produced just what they wanted.

In time, they warmed up to me. When my opportunity came to become an apprentice, none of the carpenters objected. By the end of my trial period, the engineering superintendent said that I did all that was requested of me and developed well.

During my first year as an apprentice, I performed all of the duties assigned to me and watched how the carpenters operated the various saws and shop equipment. In the second year, I began using the saws and other items, becoming more aggressive in learning and speaking my mind. The carpenters resented my growth and desire to improve my position. They wouldn't show me how to measure or cut lumber, and tried to prevent me from learning much of anything.

I didn't sit back and make up excuses about why I couldn't move up because they wouldn't teach me. I was never in the habit of letting other people determine my success. I enrolled in Galileo High School's mechanical drawing program to learn some key points I needed to master carpentry.

In public health, all work requests came in on green slips. The carpenters reviewed the slips and decided which ones they wanted to work on that day. In the third year, I felt bolder and picked up some green slips, cutting out the pieces myself. The carpenters turned me in, claiming that I was wasting lumber. That's when the superintendent called me into his office.

"Hey Cooper. I hear that you're over there wasting lumber," he said.

"Well, I'm just tryin' to learn. I'm using the lumber to practice on work orders."

He smiled (because he was that kind of guy) and replied, "Well, how are you going to learn if you don't try?"

The superintendent was a good, fair man. He didn't penalize me but wouldn't openly support me in front of the others. I could tell that he appreciated my hard work and determination to succeed. He didn't care what color I was so long as I could do the job.

At this time, I was close to getting an increase in my salary. The fourth addition to our family was here, and Joan and I now had two boys and two girls, with three of them in school.

Up the Carpenter Grade

Towards the end of my third year, the superintendent advanced me to carpenter grade WB7. Usually, you have to apprentice for at least four years before moving up to a full carpenter, which is a grade WB9, but the superintendent had other ideas.

"Here's how I'm going to do it, Coop. I'm going to move you up to WB7, so you're a little higher and can become a full carpenter, but I'm not going to take you to WB9 now because someone will complain and the civil service commission will come after me."

He kept his word. Six months later, he promoted me to WB9, and I became a full carpenter in three and one-half years instead of the required four.

The shop foreman was also a good guy. He and the superintendent weren't around the shop much but, when the foreman came in, he'd always teach me a few things. He corrected my technique whenever he could because, being self-taught, I learned many bad habits that took a few years to straighten out.

The foreman let me work on cabinet jobs. The first job—cabinets for the dental department—were long enough to stretch from one office wall to another. I don't know how I did it, but I made all of the cabinets two inches too short. The person from the dental department rejected them, but my foreman didn't get on me even though the dental department made a fuss to the superintendent.

The only thing the superintendent said to me was, "Coop, you can have those cabinets. Go make a new set for the department."

He was a fair man. I didn't get much help, but I worked hard at learning, practicing, and refining my skills. By the next year, I became an efficient and competent cabinetmaker.

Four years later, a couple of the carpenters transferred and the new ones had a different spirit. They were still all white, but they sure taught me a lot. I never blamed the other carpenters for the way they treated me because that was just the times back then. Sometimes, we'd sit around in the shop, talking and laughing, but I was different and they couldn't understand colored. They had their own beliefs about us, right or wrong.

As a colored man, I thought whites were different, too. We each did things that the other didn't understand. For example, I always lived like a miser and might have biscuits and cornbread in my lunch, and they had their nice sandwiches. I never ate around them because I didn't want them to make fun of me. At lunch, the carpenters ate in the shop and I went outside to the boiler room where the colored housekeepers ate. I guess you can say I was also discriminatory, but the carpenters, probably thinking that I was a racist, didn't know that I was only embarrassed by my lunch.

Bayview–Hunters Point

While working two full-time jobs, volunteering heavily to recruit NAACP members, and spending time with family, I somehow managed to make time for community service. For several months, I served as secretary for the Hunters Point neighborhood council, whose goal was to make the Bayview–Hunters Point area into a responsible and strong community.

Before they segregated this southeastern San Francisco neighborhood, it was a naval yard during World War II. Back in the 1940s and 1950s, coloreds left the South and flooded Hunters Point, looking for jobs and a better life. Then, when many shipyards closed down in the 1970s, Hunters Point changed from a busy, working man's place to an extremely low-income area with one of the highest crime, drug, and murder rates in San Francisco, and low goals and gross negligence in working collectively. At that time, most of the neighborhood was black.

I wanted to volunteer at Hunters Point because I knew that its people came from good southern families. They were church folks with strong morals who were stuck in the area when the jobs dried up. As each generation of children grew up in higher crime and poverty, the area kept getting worse. In the 1970s, the NAACP saw the pattern and tried to prevent our people from hurting ourselves. Ironically, at the same time, we were also telling whites that we were better than they said we were. In truth, it was hard to argue with the white man's impression of us when we had huge neighborhoods of blacks going bad. We were putting the hurt on ourselves.

Most of the Hunters Point residents lived in public housing, which made them lackadaisical. When the first generation came from the South back in the 1940s, many of them felt that their lives were so much better, compared to farming. They made 10 times more in the shipyards and thought that their children could go to any school. (This wasn't actually true; it was just that all of the schools in Hunters Point were colored schools, so it seemed open.)

Life was so comfortable compared to the farm that only a few pushed themselves enough to buy their own home. Most continued to live in public housing, letting their children run around not doing much more than sleeping and eating. These children, half-trained to expect even less from themselves, became crooks. As they grew up, they didn't work, spending most of their time hanging around, still just sleeping and eating. Young girls got pregnant, people were hooked on drugs, and black-on-black crimes and killings were out of control.

Back in the 1970s, a group of active NAACP volunteers wanted to fix this situation by starting the Hunters Point neighborhood council as our own organization. We went door to door, held family meetings, hosted social affairs and group meetings, and talked at church gatherings. We spent a lot of time teaching people and trying to guide them to a better life. We told them that they needed to do something for themselves and let them know what no one else had ever told them:

"You are better than that. You don't have to sit around doin' nothin'. Get a job. Go to school. Study your lessons."

People—sometimes large groups— came to the meetings, but they were slow to take action. I kept my hopes high and encouraged them to get administrative jobs so they could hire more of our own people who could break through the barriers.

Using the old methods, we did some good teaching in those days. We spoke wherever we could catch a crowd of people and said things that made them stronger in becoming what they hoped to be someday. We told young, married couples to put their best foot forward in providing for their families and in training their children. We said that, if they needed something, they shouldn't steal it but instead ask for it.

We emphasized how San Francisco was a fair city and that people would help them if they were trying to do something for themselves. I had learned that, if you wanted to be nothing, the city didn't care and it would let you be nothing; however, if you wanted to be something, there were always people nearby with a helping hand. With all of my ambitions, I always found someone who helped me understand where to get more information or figure out what to do.

Day after day, volunteers like me continued teaching and guiding in hopes of opening the minds in Hunters Point. We tried to open their eyes to some of our own practices, so our community would stop pushing each other down.

Taking Care of Our Own

We created much interest in turning around Hunters Point. The mayor supported us, and black policemen, community leaders, businesspeople, and church groups contributed. We were on a roll, making noise and getting our message out. One of those messages was to start trading with our own, which meant shopping at the local, black-owned businesses. Back then, there were several black-owned businesses, such as barbershops and supermarkets, in the area.

The local market wasn't getting enough business, so several of us invested in it to keep it going. It was such an important community project that Safeway sent someone to teach us how to keep fruits and vegetables fresher longer, and gave us ideas about how to run the store more efficiently. Even so, the residents still went across town to shop at the white-owned markets. When we found out the store was in trouble, we all pulled together, but it didn't work out. We became selfish and petty, arguing about doing things a certain way. Before long, the store closed.

It's disappointing our people insist on trading outside of their own. I think that part of the problem is the fact that whites have indoctrinated us since the 1700s not to trust one another. The feeling is that, if a colored man has ice, and a white man has ice, our people think that a colored person's ice isn't as cold as the white man's ice.

For everyone's hard work and dedication at Hunters Point, we hardly saw any progress. I kept my hopes high because I knew that, someday, we would be free. "Freedom" meant that blacks would have positions in high places and we could give orders like whites gave us. It meant that we could live anywhere in the city that our money would take us instead of living in our overcrowded, segregated neighborhoods.

I spent over 20 years in Hunters Point. Year after year, I volunteered but as the years passed, I kept slacking off. I got tired of working hard and not seeing any progress to show for it. No matter how hard we volunteers worked, no matter how solid the teachings, and no matter how many times people heard it at church, at home, in community groups, or at school, I couldn't see the progress I had hoped for.

Blacks back then were respectful. When we talked to them, they all agreed with our teachings, saying that they were going to keep their children from running out at night, stop them from stealing, and so on; however, when it came down to the rubber hitting the road, they didn't follow through. I didn't want to admit it, but my shrinking enthusiasm showed how I felt.

When our own people told me, "These people aren't going to change," I didn't want to believe them because I had high hopes. I blamed our volunteer group, thinking there was something we weren't doing or doing correctly. In their defense, the council mended some major issues in housing, jobs, key positions, the public school system, the political arena, voter registration, and other miscellaneous concerns; however, we did lose the long-range battle by not having the convincing teaching ability to inspire and teach young blacks to hold on to the advancements.

Hindsight lets me see how some of our biased beliefs slowed us down. One belief was that, if a child went to school and was not learning, then the teacher was not teaching. We didn't look at the family to see if they reinforced the teaching. If they made sure the child did their homework, and so forth.

I was out there, breaking my butt, talking to family after family, and trying to get these people to see the light, with no signs of progress. I learned that you can only do what you know how to do. If people don't want to change, they don't have to. Thinking I was maybe missing something in my delivery, I checked out a library book on how to lend a helping hand. As I read, I took a good look at myself and decided that I was doing the best I could.

My brother, Caleb, used to say, "You can only teach people what you know at the time to teach them. You can't go way ahead and then reach back forever through research. You just do what you do at the time you're doin' it."

Then I remembered something my younger brother, Isaiah, said, "What about you? You're always learnin' by listenin' and watchin' other people. Those people at Hunters Point have the same ability, but they're just not using it."

I couldn't argue with that. I admit that the people at Hunters Point disappointed me more than I disappointed them because I knew that they could have done better. My generation wanted to see our children become doctors, lawyers, professors, policeman, and politicians. We wanted to see that category of professionals because our generation saw so few of them. We wanted them to get those positions because we thought they could contribute more to themselves and their community. We didn't want favors; we just wanted to keep the playing field level from the inside.

After that long battle, we lost the fight. To be fair, many powerful people came out of Hunters Point. I guess that's an accomplishment, but when I look at the hundreds of thousands of people who stayed there and made the area worse, I still feel that we lost the fight. Of course, with my high goals, I expected four out of five to succeed.

Lessons and Mistakes

It took me 20 years to see the light about our people. I was still working two jobs and getting ready to volunteer when Isaiah said, "Boy, you think black can do no wrong! The very intention of a man's heart is evil, and those people, their hearts is evil. They ain't gonna do no better."

He was referring to Genesis 8:21, "And the Lord smelled a sweet savour; and the Lord said in his heart, I will not again curse the ground any more for man's sake; for the imagination of man's heart is evil from his youth."

My brother was right, but I rejected his comment and thought to myself, "What are you *talkin'* about? What do you know, telling me they can't change? I'm the guy. I'll *make* it happen."

However, I kept thinking about what he said and, after a while, I thought he might be right. When I let go of my high hopes and ego thinking, accepted the situation, and quit volunteering. I was trying to save the world, but that's kind of dumb, isn't it? I could hardly read my own name and hadn't finished grade school, but I still thought I could save the world!

For a long time, I kicked myself for being so blind and full of pride. But I don't regret any of it for all of the wonderful people I met.

That experience helped me learn a big lesson that I continue telling young people today: "You can't do for people what they must do for themselves."

It seems our people need that suppression and pressure to take action. When they can eat and have a roof over their heads, they stop pushing.

Those who came from the South thought, "Life is so much better, why rock the boat?"

During the days of slavery, colored folks said, "If your master isn't doing you too bad, don't fuss. Don't muddy the water. Just accept it and don't make waves." This mindset killed the fire to push forward and make life better for ourselves. We expect someone to hand things to us on a silver platter. If we have to reach for it, then we don't want it anymore. We're not self-motivated and need someone to lead and pull us forward.

It says in Proverbs 6:6, "Go to the ant, you sluggard, consider its ways and be wise! It has no commander, no overseer or ruler, yet it stores its provisions in summer, and gathers its food at harvest. How long will you lie there, you sluggard? When will you get up from your sleep? A little sleep, a little slumber, a little folding at the hands to rest. And your poverty will come on you like a bandit and scarcity like an armed man."

To some extent, we who thought we had our heads on straight, promoted laziness to some degree. Every time someone outside of our community said that we were damaging ourselves, we call them a racist.

As more and more blacks were getting on welfare in Hunters Point, I remember a public figure saying that making it so easy to get on welfare without making blacks responsible will only make them co-dependent. He said that we needed to get out and get a job, and stop paying young black girls to have babies. We called him a racist, thinking that we were protecting ourselves. By making excuses, we promoted our own lackadaisical attitudes and lack of appreciation. Yes, we made some mistakes. I believe welfare is a necessary method of support for some people, but some people take advantage of it.

Good Pressure

Our family had a belief that, if you didn't work for it, you didn't get it. We all had the privilege of leaving the farm, but we knew that, once we left, we were on our own. We didn't go out and come back when it got tough. We left knowing that we had to make it. Blacks need pressure to accomplish what they set out to do. If they fail, so what? Let them bite the bullet, get up, and try again stronger.

My daughter once said that people are like butterflies. If you help a butterfly break out of its cocoon, it becomes weak and then won't survive. Older folks in my community see this but not the younger generation. My grandkids don't understand this no matter how much I explain it. I blame my generation for being weak in pressuring our youngsters and not continuing the old teachings.

My generation thought the old ways were too strict, so we got soft on our kids. Over time, we got softer and demanded less, taught less, and expected less from the next generation. That was wrong.

I'm not saying we're all bad because we accomplished quite a bit and worked hard, but we should be stronger in certain areas, such as these lessons my father taught us:

"If you make a dollar, then save a dime."

"Work hard for what you want."

"Give an honest day's work for an honest day's pay."

"If you don't have your word, you don't have nothin'."

"Education creates opportunities."

Overactive

My church had many active volunteers who, like me, wanted to help advance black families. Every week, the church made several announcements of events they were holding or groups they were starting. When I'd see someone who was active, I wanted to help.

Just about every week, someone would announce, "We're gonna meet with this group on Monday. Brother Cooper, can you go?"

I didn't know how to say no. Sometimes I was overloaded, but I always made it. I still had a growing family, but I spent a lot—too much—time away from home. Joan was caring for five children almost on her own because I was busy working and volunteering.

I'd often be out all day, working my two jobs and helping others; when I came home, I just wanted to lie down. I didn't have the energy to help around the house. Then, after a few minutes, the phone would ring.

"Hey, Coop. We're goin' to the meeting. Wanna come?"

Without thinking twice, I'd run out of the house to join them.

I volunteered so much time helping other families because I held onto the hope that we were going to be free one day. Then one day, I finally came to my senses and noticed that my children were slowing down in school. That's when I said some harsh words to myself.

"Hey, Coop. You better look at home, boy! Talk about doin' all this good ... you better look at home."

I started visiting my children's schools more and making sure that they finished their lessons. I was finally practicing what I preached.

I still continued volunteering. Once in a while, Joan would say, "You spend all that time with them people. They gonna do what they want to do."

Well, I never commented, thinking she said that because volunteering just wasn't her bag and she thought I was wasting my time. Now I understand that she understood them more than I thought.

To be fair, we positively affected many lives in Hunters Point. For years, people whom I didn't recognize walked up and thanked me for helping them years back. Others would call for help because their child got in trouble. I'd tell them who to call, which was easy because not too many people helped coloreds back then. Those people always came through: If they didn't get the kid off the hook, then maybe they got the kid a lighter sentence. Either way, when the families expressed their gratitude, it warmed my heart.

Falling Apart

In the early '70s, when there were many cab robberies, we knew that blacks were doing the robbing because they only robbed white drivers. However, it didn't take long before they started robbing everybody.

That's when I knew that we blacks, as a collective group, were falling apart. There used to be an understanding among blacks that we would stand together and help our own kind. Of course, there were still crimes against each other, as there are in any society, but we mostly protected each other because no one else would.

Today, most blacks seem to believe as though people owe them something and that they shouldn't have to scratch for anything. I believe this mentality grew in the late '60s when we failed to build any hope in our children. When you teach hope, it's like a building block that keeps pushing you forward. When you struggle or people push you down, you get back up and keep going because you innately believe that you are better, deserve more, and have the ability to achieve whatever you wanted. We forgot to teach hope and now, after all these generations, the mentality is even worse.

When my siblings get together and talk about this, we say, "The Lord will give you a banana, but he's not gonna peel it."

However, most blacks today feel entitled and think, "Well, if you're gonna give it to me, you gotta bring it, peel it, and serve it."

Even when it was happening right in front of me, I couldn't see that way of thinking. In my day, if a door wasn't open, you didn't knock it down but instead just pressed it—a little now, and then a little more later. Eventually, you overcame.

Having hope and believing that I could do anything was what helped me overcome and achieve more and more every year. I flunked out of the fourth grade but kept attending night school to learn and improve myself. When I did poorly on an assignment, I stayed up just about all night to figure it out. I got in that book that I didn't understand and kept working at the problems until I got them. I didn't have any assistance; I was too selfish and shame-faced to ask the smarter students for help because I wanted to figure it out myself. I sat at my desk for hours, reading and studying. I looked at my dictionary and kept reading until I learned it.

Our Children and Hope

Our generation overcame many obstacles and made great advances, but we also lost many children. Proverbs 22:6 tells us how to teach our children when they come into the world and when they go out: "Train up a child in the way he should go: and when he is old, he will not depart from it." I began to understand where my generation went wrong. We fought to open doors for these children but, for some reason, when the doors were open, we didn't prepare them to walk through.

Their attitude was, "So what? It's an open door."

They took it for granted, not taking any responsibility or wanting to make their lives better. They just assume that the doors had been open the whole time.

If we taught them their history and the oppression their parents overcame, our people would respect each other more, and wouldn't kill and treat each other as we do. When I try to explain something to today's blacks, they get defensive and act as if I'm speaking down to them.

I learned early on that, when I'm trying to talk to them, I say, "Now I'm speaking with you," so they understand that I'm speaking on the same level.

Life in the Projects

When coloreds moved from the South to San Francisco, most lived in projects. The next generation continued living in these projects, skipping school, hanging out, and doing nothing. As long as I could get out and get a job, I always worked, but we didn't pass those values onto our children.

I would tell the younger generation, "A job is what's *happenin.'* Why don't you wanna be a supervisor?" They would respond with poor excuses for their laziness and lack of drive. No one taught them about ambition and they never fought against whites for their rights. Without ambition or an understanding of their past, each generation has less and less drive.

Colored individuals and families freed ourselves on one hand, but we enslaved ourselves on the other. We may have moved forward but, collectively, we have lost ground since the 1960s. Right now, in San Francisco, we are in worse shape—despite many more opportunities—for owning our own businesses, going to college, and being able to employ ourselves.

Our young people today feel that they deserve more than they have. They won't work for it; they want it handed to them. Several people in my generation fought hard to reach high places, but there wasn't anyone in line to keep the ball rolling and keep progress moving forward.

At one time, we broke the record for the number of qualified black principals in the San Francisco school district, and we had a black superintendent of schools who served for six years. We had the first chance to be the most successful ethnic group in America, but we let it all go. Today, we can't even keep our children in school. We also had the chance to have the first black postmaster general. We had the chance to have the first black head of the Department of Motor Vehicles…we had the chance to move ahead.

Generation after generation, we threw away our chances. We let other groups pass us by with their hard work and ambition while we sat back. The southern states benefited from the doors we opened, but it seemed as if San Francisco regressed as opportunities grew. All of the major achievements that my generation made in the '50s and '60s seem like a giant earthquake on society; then, the '70s and '80s were damaging aftershocks.

Chapter 20

Family Dreams

Cooper Family Association

By 1962, most of my siblings moved out to California, and it was a jubilant time for my family. That year, all of the west coast siblings met in Sacramento to celebrate the obstacles we overcame and achievements we made to reach California, plus the obstacles we faced settling into our new homes. We talked about borrowing money to repair cars, or paying store interest to buy furniture and other things. It wasn't easy to borrow small amounts back then or get store credit—especially if you were colored. So, when expenses came up and we needed some extra money, it was a challenge.

I asked why shouldn't we pay ourselves instead of asking for credit from a store? Why don't we borrow money from the family instead of jumping through hoops to get it from the bank? The others thought they were good ideas, so we started the Cooper Family Association.

The association was more like a membership bank. Any family member could participate so long as they paid $20 a month into the association. This built up the treasury so, when any family member needed money to purchase necessities, they could borrow it interest-free—with the understanding that they would repay the money in a timely manner so others could use it. My family elected me president, Caleb was treasurer, and Isaiah was secretary. I contributed $3,000, but I am not clear how much the others contributed.

This association was a test of our family loyalty. The monthly contributions didn't occur as consistently or often as we had expected; however, members were quick to take the money out and slow to put it back in, paying back loans $20 or less at a time. We weren't building the association as we had envisioned and, after four years, Isaiah told me that it wouldn't work unless we ruled it as a dictatorship. We three officers met and agreed that our plans for independence weren't working.

Melrose Loan and Finance

We assembled the west coast family to review our earlier plan for financial independence. After much discussion, we decided to operate as a black-owned loan and finance company. We figured that, if we were having trouble getting loans, then other upstanding blacks must have been having the same trouble.

My brother, James, and I made four trips to the Secretary of State's office in Sacramento to incorporate. Each time, they rejected the names we had selected, saying that they sounded too much like someone else's name. Eventually, we learned that the name "Melrose Loan and Finance" was available, which was the name of the area where our office stood, so we took it.

Within 45 days, we received our license and registration, with bylaws filed, as a closed corporation. We deposited $3,500 cash, left over from the Cooper Family Association, and then sold $3,500 worth of common stock to family members. We also owned $30,000 in real estate equity, which we deeded to the corporation.

At that time, I owned a duplex on Foothill Blvd. in Oakland, which I donated to the corporation, and built a small office in the front. Do you remember those cabinets I made at the Public

Health Service Hospital that were two inches too short? I put them to good use at Melrose.

I was very excited to officially open Melrose Loan and Finance for business on July 17, 1967—the only black-owned licensed loan company in northern California. I had visions of a family empire with branches in several cities, maybe even in other states. I had high hopes for our success mixed with humility and thankfulness to God for another historical event.

I thought that the colored community would applaud us for this accomplishment, but they didn't seem to care. Our opening day turnout was far less than desirable. I remember only four people stopping by, and all were family except my realtor. The rest of my siblings weren't as interested in the new corporation as I was. I never asked why, but maybe it was because the head of each family had their own jobs.

The wives pitched in as free office personnel, accepting and helping us review loan applications. My brothers Caleb and James or I stopped by daily. We got better on filtering out the riffraff and had a few repeat customers. At that time, several programs were available to help black entrepreneurs: Arthur Andersen gave us a Certified Public Accountant and Bechtel provided legal assistance—both at no cost—which motivated James to go to law school.

We solicited people from work to join our advisory board or be customers. We were building the business and trying to learn everything we could to do it right. Within a year, our younger brother Rodney agreed to help our company by becoming a CPA. Before finishing his studies, though, he got a promotion at work and dropped the CPA idea. Our other brother, Isaiah, got a law degree and passed the bar exam, becoming a valuable asset to Melrose. Our other brother, Henry, became an auto repossession mastermind. Sister Caroline and her husband were active contributors. Warren, my brother-in-law, who was married to my sister Jane, was an indispensable asset to Melrose Loan and Finance.

After 18 months, we were doing fairly well as a loan company. Our funds were limited, so we could do the typical $200 salary loan, which was profitable, and a few $500 car loans. Our advisers suggested that we sell more common stock to raise our stock distribution to $25,000. Once we did, we could sell preferred stock to investors outside of the corporation. Isaiah and I tried many avenues to increase our line of credit, but it never materialized. Our advisors suggested that we apply for a grant, but we didn't know how to write one properly. After a few months of frustrating trial and error, we were still in the same boat.

Our break finally came when Pacific Bank of Walnut Creek granted us a $10,000 line of credit, with the understanding that an auditor from their bank would check our loans every month. I applaud the branch president for giving us an opportunity. In our agreement, every good loan we made allowed us to draw on our line of credit. Banks rated good loans on the "four Cs" of credit: character, capacity, collateral, and capital. This additional line of credit helped us become financially stronger and gave us an inspirational boost towards building a profitable company.

An additional asset to building our financial business came when Pacific Bank assigned one of their representatives to monitor our company monthly.

Leadership Lessons

As president of Melrose Loan and Finance, I learned a few things about being a better manager. Once, an auditor pointed out a couple of things we did wrong when filing paperwork.

I pointed the finger, saying, "Well, I didn't know about it. That was the secretary."

The auditor answered that he didn't want to hear that. He reminded me that I was the chief of the company and, if something went on in the office that I didn't know about, then I didn't know what was going on in my own company. Boy, those words stung, but I'll never forget them because they were the truth.

I also learned that being the chief is more than being the head decision-maker. It also means that you must treat your staff well and show your appreciation for their hard work to keep them motivated. Our personnel were all unpaid family members, and

I made the mistake of expecting them to work hard just because they were family. We didn't have much money, but I could have done little things, such as having the company buy them dinner or calling a meeting to thank them.

Goodbye Civil Service

In 1973, President Nixon shut down the Public Health Service Hospital. Anyone with 25 years of civil service, regardless of age, qualified for retirement with an annuity including a 2% per year penalty for every year under 55. I was 41 years old, but I qualified with 26 years of federal service. I worked eight years in Herlong, served two years in the military, and worked 15 years in the hospital with an additional year of sick leave.

When I learned about the retirement plan, I didn't jump up and take it. I was confused because I never dreamed of retiring, especially at 41! The government was downsizing federal jobs and sending some people out of state to keep them working until retirement if they were close. I didn't want to leave San Francisco, but that's not why I took the retirement plan. At that time, my dad was visiting, and I asked him what I should do in a situation like this.

Dad answered simply, "Any money is good if you don't have to work for it." He made a lot of sense.

I took the retirement, thinking that I'd get another job. I had enough to pay back the retirement I drew out when I left Herlong, so I was in a good place. I received full retirement benefits and my house note was only $94 a month. I didn't owe anybody any money and I felt like a rich black boy!

Retiring from civil service work wasn't an easy decision for me. I found security in civil service as well as a second income. I was still driving a cab at night, but then realized that retirement would give me the opportunity to work for Melrose full time from 10 a.m. to 3:30 p.m., with occasional late evening appointments at 5 p.m.

Indoctrination

When I worked in the office, I felt all of the old indoctrination from the slave days. The black community didn't trust us, even though we didn't give them any reason not to. In their minds, black business was bad business. They thought that we were charging higher interest rates, we'd cheat them somehow, or we weren't smart enough to do the job. All they needed to do was check the numbers to know that the State of California monitored us, just like the other loan companies, but they kept believing what they wanted to believe and continued trading with the white-owned companies instead of giving us a chance.

For four years, we ran the business honestly and always passed our annual state audits. Regulations applied to us the same as any other small loan company, but, for some reason, our people didn't support us. Our money wasn't green enough, I guess.

To show you how deep the indoctrination was, Caleb and I were active members of our church—the oldest and largest black church in San Francisco, with about 1,500 parishioners at that time. We regularly opened devotionals and always volunteered for different groups and meetings. We were well known and trusted, and knew many of the parishioners by name. If one-tenth of those people had done business with us, we would have been set; however, not one came, even though we were right in their neighborhood.

I also knew hundreds of members of the NAACP in Bayview–Hunters Point, Fillmore (another San Francisco black neighborhood), and the regional office. I was an active member there for over 20 years, but not one of them came to do business with us either.

I believe that indoctrination affected my family, too. Even with our closeness and support, and our individual skills to accomplish our own goals, we could never achieve a collective goal. Deep inside, we didn't fully trust one another. If I came up with an idea and supported it wholeheartedly, the others wouldn't. They may have said yes and not made a fuss, but they wouldn't spend the time or invest the money to prove their support.

To this day, I believe there was no reason that any one of our family businesses couldn't have been successful if we had pulled together. Melrose was a closed corporation, but the family wouldn't buy its own stock. They also weren't managing their money as well as they could have by buying things they didn't need instead of investing in the company.

When I asked my family members to buy stock, they always said, "I'm gonna do it next payday," but, when payday came around, they never did it.

My mistake was not seeking advice or getting additional schooling before opening up Melrose and using my own creative plan. In life, you need to know the past before you can be successful in the present. Looking back, I realize that a knowledgeable person wouldn't have gone into business with family without having some kind of solid requirement.

I never required a commitment of either time or money from anyone. I just gave ideas, they agreed, and I started putting a lot of money and effort into it. I assumed that they would all do the same, but most didn't. By implementing a plan without wisdom, my desire to extend family assistance became an element towards making them co-dependent because they let one or two of us to do all of the work while they waited for the benefits.

Letting It Go

By working at Melrose full time, I relieved some of the wives who donated their hours, so we could put profits back into Melrose and make it stronger. I was not paid, but I still held high hopes for a strong company that would someday pay the family back handsomely.

During that time, I had the privilege of meeting many experienced professionals in the loan business, and expanding my knowledge of the loan and finance industry. We ran the business part time for the first two years, then full time for the next two years. After four years of trying, our accountant said that the only reason to be in the loan and finance business was to make a profit on our money. However, we weren't making a profit because we were paying 2% over the prime interest rate for the money we were using. That would have been all right if our customers repaid their loans in a timely manner. As it was, we made 30% on our $200 loans, and 21% on $500 to $700 loans, but our customers took too long repaying them.

At that time, savings accounts made 8% interest, so our advisors recommended that we leave behind all of the expenses and headaches of running Melrose and just put our money into a straight savings account. I counseled with Isaiah about winding down the company before telling the other stockholders, who weren't contributing any time, financial investment, or energy into the company.

Without judgment, I realized and accepted the fact that the family owners of the Melrose Loan and Finance could not elevate their thinking from being slave consumers to powerful suppliers. As a child, I always wanted our family to stay and grow together; then, as an adult, my desire turned into great visions of pooling our collective talents to grow a business empire.

I had a difficult time letting Melrose go because I really thought that this was it! I thought Melrose would be the first successful corporation from the family. I experienced as much sadness at our closure as I experienced joy on opening day. After filing the necessary paperwork, we collected 95% of our outstanding loan payments in the mail over the next two years. In the end, we salvaged a small profit.

We received a personal property broker license, which we received from the State of California's Department of Corporations. We held on to that license for two years after the closure. Then Secretary of State charged an excessive fee for our business license, regardless of whether that license was active. With that law in effect, we mailed the license to the Secretary of State and registered ourselves as an inactive loan and finance.

Repeating History

After Melrose, I should have learned my lesson, but I kept trying to get the family working together in a business. I donated the

Melrose building to the family, so I thought we could all pool our money together and purchase more properties as rentals and other investments.

As it turned out, we didn't buy another property together until much later. Some time in between, though, we picked up a property in Sacramento, near Fell Street, for only $250—the whole house and the lot. It was a gift from God. At just $250, we could have charged a dollar a month for rent and still have made a profit.

It was our first rental, and Micah was supposed to manage it since he lived in Sacramento. Unfortunately, he let in some renters who tore up the property so badly that no family member would help us repair it. Caleb and I were so disgusted by the damage and lack of help, we walked away from the house and the lot. We didn't owe anything on it, and I don't know what happened to it afterwards. We never looked at the lot again.

As if that weren't enough, I tried the family business idea again. This time, we owned a service station in Sacramento, which was a good deal because Micah was a first-class mechanic. We could also make money selling gas and a few items in the sundry store. All the money that Micah would make working on cars would go back to the family account and the company would pay him a good salary.

The problem was that Micah was a player. Yes, he was a very good mechanic, but he didn't like getting his hands dirty. He didn't show up for work regularly, and we couldn't get the others to look at the station or help.

Caleb and I showed up religiously on our days off to work at the station, but that wasn't enough to keep it open. Micah could have run the entire place himself if he would have just shown up regularly. We blew that business in a short time. It was a shame because that service station was too good to be true. We had to pay a percentage of the gas we sold, and the rest belonged to us. The Lord blessed us with so many opportunities, but I guess we wanted Him to come down and run the businesses, too.

It took four failed family businesses before I realized some important lessons. Each of my siblings was a strong leader individually and in their own profession, but our fate was not to pool our skills to grow a family corporation. I tried to make the family work together because I learned that a group could do more than individuals could. Maybe it was because, as farmers, we had to work together to survive, and that may have started my desire to work together in a family business. From that point, however, I respected their independence and stopped dreaming of collective business ideas.

One of my other big life desires did happen, though. I wanted all of my siblings to have a good education, and they all did. Several of them got well-paying jobs and kept moving up from there. I'm proud of all of my siblings for what they achieved for their own families.

Regrouping

When it came to setting goals, I always aimed for the sun with the expectancy of falling lower to the moon. I felt incredible joy every time I achieved a goal, and kept high expectations of greater joy every time I set another goal. Each time I achieved another goal, my happiness felt maximized.

My only regret is not taking the time to enjoy my day-to-day happiness more, such as playing cards, going to ball games, visiting parks, skating with church groups, and going to the movies. In my Herlong days, I could have taken more for lunch than a couple pieces of cornbread. As long as I can remember, I have been so busy scrimping and saving and working and volunteering and planning that I forgot to let myself enjoy who I am and where I was. I was so busy looking for the happiness that would come later, that I ignored the happiness in front of me. Looking back, I see that satisfaction doesn't come only when you achieve your goals; it also comes from enjoying the journey along the way.

After Melrose closed, I only had one job—driving a cab at night—and volunteered less with Hunters Point. For the first time since I was a young boy, I had free time on my hands. I was feeling a little tired from the constant go, go, go over the last several years. I vowed to take three months off and enjoy myself hunting, fishing, and going to the movies—just hanging around and being satisfied with working one job.

Tricked in My Cab

A month into my grand plan, I was robbed while driving my cab not too far from home. One evening, shortly after 10 p.m., I got a radio call to pick up a passenger on Excelsior and Mission Streets. When I arrived, I saw a black male standing outside, looking like he had a bad right leg. As I got out of the cab to help, I pointed to the front seat.

He said, "No, I want to sit in the back."

I didn't think anything of it and helped him get in. I walked around the back of the cab, and got behind the wheel, intending to say, "Where to, sir?"

Instead, when I turned to look over my shoulder, the barrel of a gun was pointing at my face. I looked around and saw another black man, waiting in a car nearby. That's when I realized I fell for an obvious trap.

I had always prided myself as an experienced driver but, this time, they tricked me. I should have known when the passenger insisted on getting in the back of the cab. In all of my years driving, anyone with a hurt leg always wanted to sit up front because it had more room.

When I would hear that another driver was robbed, I'd think to myself, "You ain't gonna make me drive you in no dark alley and rob *me*!"

My robber saw my money pouch, sitting beside me in plain view, and shouted, "Give me your money and *don't move!*"

I could tell that he was inexperienced. Inexperienced robbers killed many drivers while running around for fixes, so I talked my way through the whole thing, trying to keep him calm.

As quietly as I could, I said, "Sir, I can't give you my money and don't move. I'm sitting still as I ain't breathing hardly. Would you reach over and get my money? It's sittin' right over there."

He thought it was a good idea, so he reached over and took the money pouch. He flipped through it, taking all $30 out, then asked, "You got some more money? Where's your wallet? Give me your wallet and *don't move!*" Every sentence ended with, "Don't move!"

I was still totally cool; I didn't get scared until later. I quietly said, "Sir, I can't get my wallet and don't move. It's in my back pocket. Could we slide out and then can you get it out of my pocket?"

He thought that was a good idea, too. "Yeah, but you better not try nothin'!"

After he grabbed my wallet, he said, "Hold out your hand!"

He snatched my watch off my wrist before he took off in the waiting car.

After he left, I radioed in and told them about the robbery. The police came quickly and got my report. Of course, Yellow Cab told me to put the car back into the garage and, once I did that, they let me go home. During the days following the robbery, I became suspicious and jumpy every time I picked up a passenger.

A Union Man

After 15 years of driving swing shift for Yellow Cab, I ended the adventure. In a matter of months, I went from having two jobs and a company to having no job and no company.

I decided to fall back on my carpentry skills. In my time, it was hard to get a job because unions were strong. If you weren't a union member, they wouldn't hire you because the unions would come out and picket the site, and nobody wanted that.

I asked various people whom I knew about getting into carpentry. "What's it like workin' for the union? How do I get in the carpenters union?"

Following their advice, I joined Carpenters Local Union Number 22, located on Fillmore Street in San Francisco. Within five days, they accepted me in as a journeyman carpenter. For the next two days, I went into the union hall, reporting for roll call.

When my number came up, I got a job working on the West Portal tunnel.

This job was different from anything that I experienced at Public Health Service Hospital. I couldn't understand what the foreman was telling me to do, and spent three days fumbling until they sent me packing with a farewell check. When you don't measure up on construction jobs, the foreman gets your check from the office and hands it to you. There's no write up or papers to fill, like civil service jobs.

I returned to the union hall, waiting for my number to come up again. I was fortunate because there were so many construction jobs in those days, I never waited too long. Over the next four months, I got three jobs, each one lasting three to six days. Although I made $15 per hour, it didn't provide enough security because, each time I left the union hall, I never knew when I'd work again. The union required that there had to be a certain number of blacks on a job so, if there were five carpenters, one of them had to be black—like the pepper in the salt. It was a federal affirmative action law, not a union rule.

During my days off, I went back to school, trying to learn more. I had so much schooling that I got sick of myself. However, I always held on to the belief that I could do better to prepare myself to reach my goals.

It took me about 12 to 15 months before I learned how to work in the union system. When the union laid you off, carpenters could work at any jobsite. Before the union job ended, we would ask the foreman if he needed a worker somewhere else. By adopting this method, I could find another job that may last a few days or a couple of weeks.

Union construction jobs were a lot more challenging than cabinetmaking and finishing work, but that just meant that I needed to apply my usual determination with greater force. I kept my eyes and ears open, observing and learning everything I could at each jobsite. I only asked questions when I thought I could learn how to do something more efficiently. I showed up every day on time and worked hard for eight hours a day. Rain or shine, I never let up on my performance, letting the foreman decide when it was time to quit.

A few years later, I landed a union job with a large concrete company, working on high-rise buildings. One was the 15-story wing of UCSF Medical Center on Parnassus Avenue, replacing the old Langley Porter Psychiatric Institute and the Moscone Convention Center (named after George Moscone, the city mayor murdered by a city supervisor). That job lasted over three years, which allowed me to work on several new jobsites and learn more about carpentry and other skills like teamwork.

I continued working as a union carpenter for the next 15 and one-half years before deciding to retire—again. I became proficient during that time, and used the colloquial carpenter's language, such as referring to houses as "matchboxes."

My home-building skills enabled me to build my sister Aaliyah's dream home in Reno. In that house, she raised her family and enjoyed a number of year before she died.

I was also proud of using my skills to fulfill another one of Aaliyah's desires. Next to her home, she purchased a lot, hoping to build our mother a house there. Aaliyah hired her church's deacon to oversee the building project. A contractor built the concrete block foundation and the family did the rest. Caleb lived in Salt Lake City at the time, but he came to help along with Aaliyah and her sons. I visited from San Francisco to serve as chief carpenter. In four months, we built a comfortable three-bedroom, two-bathroom house for Mom. Dad wouldn't leave the South and his own home, so Mom experienced her own freedom and adventure.

Mom moved from Louisiana and settled into her new house, living up her independence and learning new ways. She was in her 70s at the time, and taught herself how to drive, became active in a local church, and made new friends everywhere she went. She adjusted to her new life well and enjoyed many years in her new home until the Lord came and took her away. I am happy that she had those years there and sad that she's no longer with us.

Chapter 21

Leave Something Behind

Helping or Hurting?

With all of the new carpentry skills I learned on the union jobs, I started to buy fixer-upper homes here and there, thinking that I was going to own the world. As usual, I had no real plan. I bought based on where family was, thinking that I could help them by providing affordable housing while building up the family wealth at the same time.

I thought it would be a good idea to buy rundown HUD (U.S. Department of Housing and Urban Development) properties, fix them up, and rent them as investment income. I fixed up one property after another, the whole time thinking how it would help my family. However, I didn't see was how I was hurting them—especially my children. By now, our fifth child was born—a daughter—we had two boys and three girls.

Similar to what I did at Hunters Point, I hurt people by intervening, thinking that I was going to make things better. I thought I was helping and giving them an opportunity to stand stronger. Now I see that my efforts only enabled people until they lost what little desire they had to succeed. Sometimes, the best way to help is by doing nothing.

I still regret one instance where I learned that some organization was giving away free turkeys that day to needy families. I called up a single mom with four boys whom I knew at Hunters Point.

"Look, you short on money," I told her. "You can go down, get a turkey, and save $4 or $5," which was a lot of money in those days.

Later that night, right when I was in bed and ready to fall asleep, she called.

"Brother Cooper, could you go get that turkey for me?"

I should have said no. She had four boys who had the whole day to go down there, and it was so close that they could have walked there to pick it up. What did I do? I got out of bed in the middle of the night and picked up that turkey for her!

After that, I said to myself, "Cooper, you gotta wake up and smell the coffee."

How stupid could I be? When people like that are in the habit of using you, they'll use you. You think you're helping them, but you're not.

So many times, I let people use me or I tried to help so much that I ended up pushing the person further down—even with my own children. Sometimes, I think about it and don't feel too proud of myself. Some things I still hold against myself for being so dumb. Some things I get to chuckling about, thinking how the Lord will not forget your kind deeds as long as you benefit others. However, the Lord must look at me sometimes and shake His head.

My Biggest Lesson

Joan and I always told our children that they could be anything they wanted to be—the sky was the limit! Even so, I will never know what they all could have achieved because I infringed on their development. I taught my children to be strong, yet, when they went out and did things, I intervened, thinking that I was making their lives a little easier. I fooled myself and tried to control the situation. I forgot my own valuable lesson: You can't do for people what they must do for themselves.

When my oldest daughter became of age, she got a job, moved into a decent neighborhood, and paid her own rent—happy as she could be. My second daughter progressed in the same manner and got a good job working with computers, paid her own rent, and even bought herself a car. They were both accomplished young ladies and we were proud of them.

By then, I had bought three homes from HUD, refurbished them, and was looking for renters. I convinced my oldest daughter to move into the house in Richmond, thinking that it was a good deal, because she would only pay $350 per month rent, which was $50 less than what she was paying. By living in one of my houses, she could also contribute to the family collective.

After some pushing, she agreed. Within a few months of moving in, she lost her drive and self-worth. She got involved with the wrong crowd and starting going downhill. I didn't know it at the time, but hindsight tells me that it was because I infringed in her life.

I went off and did it again with my second daughter. She finally agreed to live in one of my HUD houses and was doing all right until her car needed work. She tried a few mechanics who didn't help much.

"I know a guy," I told her, "who can fix this and do a lot better job!"

The cotton-pickin' guy ended up taking the car apart and never got it back together. She ended up with a big bill and no car. That's when she started to lose her drive and got involved with drugs.

Sometimes, I realized where I went wrong and say to myself, "Cooper, you ignorant guy! Why did you do somethin' like that? You know better. *Why did you do that?* You taught 'em everything and they knew how to handle it. Then you came around and messed it all up!"

My oldest son always stayed focus and remained gainfully employed until his retirement. When he was starting out, trying to support his family, I offered help.

"Here's a little place you can rent that'll save you money," I said.

He seemed to do all right, using that help as a step up, but my other children didn't follow.

Over the next few years, my second son followed his sisters' pattern, using drugs to march to the beat of nothingness. When I first suspected that he was taking drugs, I was in denial for about three months. I would come home and see at least four or five of his friends hanging around in the house, but I never asked any questions.

One day, I caught them with a shoebox full of marijuana. I didn't know what it was, but I knew it didn't smell like regular cigarettes, and grabbed the box.

"Whatever this is, you're not going to have it in *my* house!" I dumped the contents of the box into the commode and flushed it down. My son insisted that it wasn't his and that his friends had brought it over, so I told him that I would not allow those children in the house anymore. I wanted to believe that was the end of it.

I closed my eyes and thought, "*My* son wouldn't hang out with kids like that. *My* son wouldn't take drugs!"

For the next six months, I ignored the other clear signs that he and my daughters were taking drugs. I purposely stayed in denial and fooled myself into pretending that all was under control. I did not want to believe that my kids could act like the people whom I spent years teaching in Hunters Point. I told myself that my kids were taught right … my kids knew better … my kids had a strong foundation. I looked the other way and beat myself up with self-pity. I felt mostly disappointment because I expected *my* children, above everyone else's, to be on top of the ladder.

Even in denial, a part of me couldn't ignore the truth. I kept saying to myself, "Boy, your children is takin' drugs … your children is takin' drugs."

I had to say it to myself many times because I didn't want to believe it. When I finally opened my eyes, it became personal.

I asked myself, "Why would *my* children take drugs? Why would *my* children want to do this when they can be anything they want to be? I gave them every opportunity to go to school, set goals, and know how to make the right decisions that would keep them on track. Why would they throw it all away?"

I thought that my strict discipline would prevent my children from straying. When my youngest son was about 12 years old, his teacher called me, saying that he was giving her a bad time and she couldn't discipline him. That night, I sat him down.

"Don't you have that teacher call me again at work and say that you bein' disrespectful!"

A week or two later, the teacher called again with the same problem. I left the job and beat his butt—at school. After that, no teacher had any more trouble from him in that sense, but he was lackadaisical about turning in his homework and couldn't learn his lessons. I sat down to help him with his lessons a few times, but I felt like giving up.

One time, I was sitting in a parent-teacher meeting when the principal said, "Well, you can't make a racehorse out of a jackass."

We all laughed about it, but he was right. If my son wanted to be a jackass, he was going to be a jackass. Naturally, I kept trying to make him into a racehorse because I knew it was in him, but I didn't know how to get him there. All of my children knew that, when I told them to do something, I meant it. So, when my children decided not to make their lives what they ought to be, I felt as if they were purposely disobeying me.

I let myself have a pity party for a minute, but not more. As my family would say, "Anything that happened in the past is like water poured in the sand." I knew I couldn't get that water back, so I got out of the pity party and figured out what to do next.

I realized that the best thing was to leave them alone and let them figure out their own way. This forced me to practice "tough love"—something I should have done years before. I think they came up with the phrase because it's tougher for the parent than the child. I spent many years enabling them under the misconception that I was helping them, and I knew I now had to let them stand on their own.

Thinking back, this may be how my dad felt when we moved out to the west coast, one by one. We were a very amenable family, always listening to our parents and doing what they told us to do.

Even so, my dad wanted us to be farmers and none of us became one. I didn't learn this until years later after I had my own family. He must have thought we were crazy, getting civil service jobs and working in offices. We didn't live the farmer's life my father wanted for us, but we still live his teachings. If you sat down and talked to anyone of my brothers and sisters now, you would see that they put into practice what he taught us and what my mom reinforced.

Tough Love

Kindness comes under the umbrella of love and care, which hides a multitude of faults. Kindness helps families and society tolerate one another, but with kindness comes a little blindness when you close your eyes to the negative and focus on the positive. You must use tough love to provoke improvement, not promote lackadaisical attitudes. Tough love is tough to practice, but you must practice it. It means you must take a stand and speak out. You must abide by what you say, regardless of how you feel. I've shed many a tear as a man, especially for my girls. The boys could stand out in the rain for all I cared, but it was tough for the girls.

When they were still addicted, I told my girls that they couldn't come inside my house. One rainy day, they came by, begging and crying, but I held firm. Can you imagine how difficult it is to keep your daughters out in the cold rain? I had to do it, and I'll tell any caregiver that, if you want your children to hear what you are saying, you need to do just that.

You didn't make your children disobey what you taught them; they decided to do that with their own free will. If you tell them that they can't come into your house, you make sure they don't.

However, a couple of times, when the weather was very bad, I told them, "Look, I'm going to get you a motel room for a night or two, but you can't come to the house, you hear? If you come back like this again, I don't care about the weather. You can sleep under a tree."

If you ever practice tough love, don't *ever* break your word. Once you do, you lose. While you're going through the dark times,

you don't know if you're doing the right thing. You just need to
stick it out and pray for the best. Much later, my daughters told
me many times how grateful they were that I turned them away.
They thanked me for practicing tough love because it saved them.
When you're a caregiver practicing tough love, do not look for
applause or expect anyone to tell you that you're doing the right
thing, but you must have family support.

I talked to my son who was doing well on his own, "Look, if I
say that your sisters can't come in here, I expect your support. You
can't let 'em in your house either because, if you do, you're not
helping them. If you disobey, then we won't speak either."

At the same time, I realized that someone in my family might
take in my daughters, saying that they could stay for a minute, but
then they would need to get their act together. So, after warning
my son not to take his sisters in, and then finding out that he did,
I tolerated it. I didn't punish them too severely because if we both
put them out, and something happened to them, I'd never forgive
myself.

When there's trouble, family has to stick together. I suppose
that's what happened when I ran away from the farm. My aunt
and uncles didn't have to take me in, but I think they had so much
respect for my dad that they let me stay for a little while, thinking
that I'd come to my senses soon enough. They probably thought
that, if they turned me away and I got hurt, then they'd let down
my dad.

Choosing and Asking

Through those difficult years, I learned that, once children
become of age and go out on their own, they choose good or evil.
The same is true for what I teach because they have the choice to
adopt those lessons or ignore them.

My dad taught a lesson, which came back to me many times
over the years: "If you know someone who's got information and
you want it, but you don't ask for it, it means that you don't want
it."

Once, when my youngest son had diabetes and serious kidney trouble, I told him, "I'll take you to a trusted black doctor and a trusted white doctor, so you'll get it in black and white! I'll get the best information I can find, and it's up to you to use it. When you've got that before you, and you still go on draggin' and draggin' and don't ask, it means that you don't want it."

My father taught us that, "Whatever problem you have, it shouldn't be so bad that you can't ask my opinion if you need it. You know that I will not give you a prima facie decision if I don't know. I will seek the answer."

He was serious and, through the years, I was just as serious in teaching my children and grandchildren the same thing. I look back now and say that, through all I've received from them, it's been gratifying. Even with the tears I've shed, what they've given me outweighs all the negative parts and all of the challenges were worth it.

Returning to Real Estate

Watching my children lose themselves in drugs made me give up for the first time in my life, and I felt as if I had hit bottom, too. Sometimes, the situations got so dark that I thought there was surely no hope for them. For a 12-month period of practicing tough love, I stopped buying houses. I didn't have the energy or interest to do anything anymore.

In time, my faith in God helped me pull myself together and focus on my goals with new eyes. Proverbs 13:22 tells us to leave our children something: "A good man leaveth an inheritance to his children's children: and the wealth of the sinner is laid up for the just." You may not feel they deserve it, but leave them something anyway because God has a plan for them and you're responding to God with His plan.

In two families in my neighborhood, I saw the benefits of that lesson. One was a couple with two boys who were lazy and always getting in trouble; it seemed as if they weren't even worth taking the time to beat. When the parents died, they left the boys their house. The boys kept the house up, paid the house taxes on time, and took care of it. If the parents hadn't left them the house, they would be out on the street.

I kept thinking about that scripture until it helped me start to buy and fix up houses again. This time, I bought them as an investment *for me*. I was the sole proprietor of this adventure as a landlord. If I knew a family member who benefited from my properties, that was a bonus, but it was no longer the focus. Another reason I kept buying houses was because I wanted to prepare myself for what my children would need. I knew that, when they straightened out, they would need a place to stay. I went back to my old belief of being prepared to help my children and other people in my life. The thought of being rich didn't fuel my drive, but I always wanted to be able to give a helping hand.

When we were kids, we were taught if you're in a ditch, and your brother's in a ditch, you can't help each other. One of you has to get out and pull the other one up. Neither of you may be in a ditch now, but if you both keep walking down the same road, that's where you'll end up. One of you needs to walk a different road.

Later on, I tried to solicit my children as real estate partners, but only my oldest was interested. We bought a property together and sold it two years later. He wisely reinvested his profits into something very important—his family home. I could not get him to partner with me again; it's just not his bag, I guess. Through my years purchasing property, I acquired many assets (not counting the house in Sacramento I purchased for $250 and walked away from):

1958:Single-family Junior 5 (a two-bedroom, two-bath home) in San Francisco for $15,500, my family's first home and where I still live. Over the years, I added four more bedrooms and three full bathrooms.

1960s:Duplex in Oakland for $18,500. I later donated it to the family for the Melrose Loan and Finance (later called FAMCO).

1978:Two-bedroom, one-bathroom home with a basement in Richmond for $8,000.

1979:Vacant lot on the right side of the above Richmond house for $2,586.

1980s:Single-family home with two bedrooms, one bathroom, and a detached garage and mother-in-law unit in Oakland for $38,000.

1980s:Single-family home, converted it to three bedrooms and one bathroom, with a small living room and a full kitchen in Oakland for $18,500.

1981:House on the left side of the above Oakland home for $15,000.

1995:Two lots with four separate buildings (like a miniature commune) in San Francisco for $76,000, built in 1925 and in good shape. The front house had two bedrooms, one bathroom, a basement, and a carport; the second had one bedroom and one bathroom with no basement; the third was a studio; and the fourth was like a shotgun house with one bedroom, one bathroom, and a single-car garage in the front.

1998:Duplex in Sacramento for $76,000. Each unit had two bedrooms, one bathroom, and a large common space around the unit. I repaired each unit myself to meet building code requirements before renting it out, and still manage and repair the properties.

2004:Townhouse with two bedrooms, one bathroom, a dining room, and a kitchen in Sacramento for $41,000.

2004:Townhouse with five bedrooms, two full bathrooms, a kitchen, a dining room, a laundry room, and a small outside yard in Sacramento for $121,000.

2004:Single-family home with five bedrooms and three full bathrooms on over 1 acre, plus an additional 7/8th-acre adjacent lot, for $280,000.

2006:Single-family home with three bedrooms, two bathrooms, and a two-car garage in San Francisco for $400,000. I added a full mother-in-law quarter downstairs.

A Good Life after All

As I kept purchasing one property after another, I considered it a skill that I developed over the years. I used common sense in purchasing good deals, paying in full, and letting the equity build without touching it. I still think that I didn't live up to my potential, but the progress I made with each home purchase was gratifying. I lessened my overhead expenses by taking out loans on two Oakland and two San Francisco properties. If I considered myself miserly before, I became even more of a spendthrift for a period afterwards.

When I was acquiring properties, I thought that, when I got all of the properties I wanted, I'd be happy—running all over the country, seeing the sites, and visiting my family and friends—but that didn't happen. I still live in my same old house and I don't leave the city much. For my rentals, I won't hire anyone to do the work, so I fix everything myself.

My brothers have to remind me to give myself credit for all I've accomplished. I own several properties throughout northern California, but I can't see that it's a big accomplishment. I figured that, if I could do it, anyone could. However, when I sit back and think about all I have, I'm living well. It took me a long time to do it, but I admit that it's a good life.

When my dad visited before he returned to the Lord in 1978, I owned three properties. I showed him the buildings and he looked around a little, not saying anything or showing any emotion. I'm sure he was proud of his children, and finally concluded that it was a blessing we all left the farm. He never expressed it; however, knowing him the way I do, I'm sure he was proud. I'm glad that when we visited home as adults, we made sure Dad knew how much his children appreciated him and his teachings.

Following or Leading

Since I was a child, and even now, I feel that helping others is part of my calling. If you don't give a helping hand, then what good is all of the stuff you've acquired? I recognize that I've had many blessings myself and had much help given to me. You don't get blessings just for you; you get blessings so you can bestow blessings to others.

My mom used to teach us a saying: "Cast your bread upon the water and it will return." It meant, do your good deeds and they will come back to you.

I heard many sayings from the old folks that we children never understood until adulthood, like "Every tub sits on its own bottom."

That saying is my whole life lesson in many ways, meaning, "Everybody must take responsibility for themselves."

Sometimes, when I hear younger people complain about old folks not knowing what they're talking about, I say to them, "Look here. If you knew one-tenth of what they know, and with no book learnin' in a sense, you'd be sittin' on top of the world."

I can think of many sayings the old folks used that have come true. If we had practiced what they taught us, none of us would have this common problem of our children running out and getting into trouble, then running back to us for help. It doesn't mean that we shouldn't give them a helping hand. The problem with most parents is that they *hold* their children's hands! You've got to *let go*!

My parents taught us that, if you love your children, there are certain things you will not do to harm them, and, if they love themselves, there are certain things they won't do to harm themselves.

I always ask my grandchildren and great-grandson, "Do you love yourself?"

"Oh, yeah, *yeah*!"

"Then how you doin' in school?"

"Well, I, uh …"

I'd ask again, "Do you love yourself? Well, you gotta be able to compete. Do you wanna be a leader or a follower? Do you wanna be the one taking orders or the one giving orders? That tells you how well you love yourself."

Chapter 22

The Journey

Learning about Drugs

By 1997, I put in nearly 16 years in the carpenters union. I had just finished a job and was going to sign up for another, when it suddenly hit me.

"Cooper, why are you *doin'* this? You don't need the work. It's time to quit."

As quickly as that idea came to me, I retired for the second time at age 65. I devoted my free time to traveling through Louisiana, seeing my hometown and other nearby towns and cities where friends and relatives still lived. I enjoyed sojourning through this land, reminiscing about the past and appreciating all that had happened since I left.

After a short period of feeling fully retired for the first time in my life, I thought about selling insurance. For years, I carried a California life and disability agent license and thought it would be an exciting new occupation. I tried it for a short time and decided that I didn't want to be an agent.

I may have been retired, but I still liked to learn. The one question that still raged through my mind was, "Why do people turn to drugs?"

At one time, four of my children, and my nieces and nephews, were on drugs, and it had damaged just about every family I knew. I began to hate people, which was an awful feeling. I didn't feel good about myself for it, but I had no love for people using drugs.

I have always carried the belief that when you don't understand something, you should learn something about it. After all my years taking assorted classes, I raised myself to a twelfth-grade level. I looked at several community and state colleges for college-level courses that would answer my questions about drug addiction. Laney College in Alameda had a package where you could earn a certificate on illicit drugs and move up to an associate degree.

I enrolled in an "Illicit Drug Use" course in spring 1997, excited to be a full-time college student at 65 years old! I had taken several classes from Laney in the past:

- Fundamental Drafting/Techniques (Fall 1976)
- Blueprint Reading (Fall 1993)
- Public Speaking (Spring 1994)
- Voice (Fall 1994)

My class was a field-experience course where you went to the drug users in recovery centers. I chose Glide Memorial Church between Ellis and Taylor Streets in San Francisco, a drug-heavy area. I applaud Glide and its founder, Cecil Williams, because he had enough foresight to understand how deeply drugs damage society. Glide was San Francisco's first rehabilitation and outreach center, feeding and training its people to get their lives back on track, and a perpetual asset to those in need of a helping hand.

Glide teaches residents these creeds to remain faithful and resist drugs:

1. Gain control over my life
2. Tell my story to the world
3. Stop lying
4. Be honest with myself
5. Accept who I am

6. Feel my real feelings
7. Feel my pain
8. Forgive myself and forgive others
9. Practice rebirth and a new life
10. Live my spirituality
11. Support and love my brothers and sisters

With my experience meeting different personalities in the military and while driving a cab, talking to these recovering drug users surpassed them all. They were open to answering my questions and seemed to take pleasure in exposing their weaknesses. However, after forcing myself to attend two semesters at Glide, I couldn't handle it any longer. The people and their stories were too much for me. Rather than give me much insight about people, I felt more disgusted by them. After Glide, I found another agency, which felt more normal, and completed my final fieldwork semester.

My New Addiction

To earn a certificate of completion in illicit drugs, I completed the following courses:

Spring 1997: 9 units of field experience; 3 units each of Group Dynamics, Families in Crisis, and Human Development, working with small groups

Fall 1997: 3 units each of Self-development, Community Resources, Communications, and Advanced Self-help

Spring 1998: 3 units each of Health Education and Social Psychology of Substance Abuse, and 4 units of English 1A

Fall 1998: 3 units each of Psychology Pharmacology of Drugs, Counseling Skills, and Law & Substance Abuse

Spring 1999: 3 units each of Group Dynamics, Family in Crisis, and Adult Development
Fall 1999:   3 units each of Introduction to Biology, Human Values, African American Writers, Computer Literacy, and Elementary Algebra.

When I finished all of my classes, I was so close to earning an associate's degree that I decided to go for it. I continued learning because I still wanted to know more about why people would put drugs in their body. I learned that, once they started drugs, it had drawing power. That helped me understand people a little better and tolerate them a little more. They still shouldn't have taken drugs in the first place, but I understood better that, once they made that bad choice, the drugs started to control them.

I learned that there are two kinds of drug users: those who try it, like it, and walk away from it; and those who try it and become addicted. The addicts are the ones who give you the most trouble because they start killing and stealing.

School is sort of like an addiction, too. I started learning and I wanted to keep going. I earned my illicit drugs certification at the same time I earned my first associate's degree in counseling substance abuse. When I walked across the stage during graduation, I rejoiced in the glory of graduating after pushing myself to learn at 68 years old. I couldn't tell which I enjoyed more: the reward of graduation or seeing so many family members supporting me. I will cherish that memory, and the graduation ring they gave me, for the rest of my life.

Then, I was so close to a general education degree, I signed on for another semester. I passed elementary algebra only by the grace of God. After a few more classes, I earned my second associate's degree in elementary education—at almost 70 years old! Still addicted to education, I nearly signed up for a bachelor of art's degree, thinking that it would be just a few more classes, but I caught myself and stopped.

Selling Drugs

In addition to earning my degrees, I'm proud of my punctual dedication. I attended six semesters in succession, and was late for one class because I miscalculated traffic, and left one class early.

President Barack Obama tells Americans, "Yes, we can!"

I say to myself, "Yes, I can!"

Speaking as one who has traveled through this world of adventure and discovery, I learned that becoming addicted to books isn't negative because there is so much information with which to feed the mind with warmth and excitement. After my second associate's degree, I weaned myself from school by convincing myself that it was time to help those in need and apply my school learning to the real world.

I volunteered at a drug rehab unit under the court system and promoted by the City of San Francisco. At the time, first offenders caught selling drugs usually got two years in jail. The judge sometimes gave the offenders an option where they could spend a certain number of months in jail and a certain number of months in a group rehab class, or do community service. To stay out of jail, the offender had to do two things: check in and go to class. But these people would forfeit the grace extended to them. They would miss class and not call, they'd show up late, or they showed up and never paid attention.

I spent six months talking to offenders about their future and the consequences of the life they were choosing. Many of the courts' clientele were black with little or no motivation. Their reply was that what they were doing was acceptable. Their responses confirmed what's written in Judges 17:6, "In those days there was no king in Israel, but every man did that which was right in his own eyes." This was about how a man's ways always seem right to him. Many of these offenders came from church-going families like mine, but their parents failed to follow Proverbs 22:6, "Train a child in the way he should go." Meaning, have your child take responsibility for his actions.

For instance, I knew one of the offenders and his mother. They were tenants of mine at one time and were always struggling. His mother knew that her son was selling drugs, but she didn't make him take any responsibility and she looked the other way. When I saw the boy in the rehab unit, I talked to him.

"Boy, what in the world are you *doin*? You got nerve to sell drugs to your own kind! Look, I don't hate nobody bad enough to sell drugs to 'em. I might sell him some strychnine 'cuz that take him out right now, but do you know this stuff messes up a person's mind in a way that's worse than being dead?"

He argued, "Well, if I don't, somebody else will."

When I admitted that my children were using drugs, I wouldn't let them in the house, but I don't know if they sold them. I said, "I don't applaud you usin' them, but if you sellin' them, you worse than the worse kind of criminal to me, 'cuz you selling that stuff to your own kind, or to human beings period, ruinin' their mind. When a person's mind is gone, that's it. If you do it to someone else, you gonna do it to me. I don't want you around here."

I'm not pointing any fingers and I accept what I, as a parent, failed to do, which allowed my children to go wayward. I plead guilty. I believe that most of us are sincere, loving parents, hoping the best for our children and sacrificing greatly for them, but we do not hold them responsible for their actions. We talk about other children selling drugs and the fact that we don't want them around but, if our child does it, we find a way to make excuses for their actions.

The Power of Moms

One of my college teachers said that mothers could solve many of the problems we have in this community by making their children take responsibility for what they do. Mothers could turn around bad language, boys mistreating the girls, drug use, gangs, crime ... nearly every major social problem we have.

Mothers could turn their communities around, if they wanted, by pulling together. If mothers could see that, when their son calls his girlfriend b****, he's calling his mamma the same thing.

When a boy slaps a girl, moms justify it by saying, "Oh, she ain't no good." The mother doesn't understand that she's condoning a man slapping her around, too. That's how negative behavior becomes acceptable and gets worse in every generation.

Mothers have the power to stop our community's self-destruction and turn it all around. Women are strong. History proves that they don't need no cotton pickin' men. During World War II, women ran the country by taking over factory jobs and working on the farms. If they could do it then, under extreme duress, why couldn't they do it now?

In my day, the woman ran the house. Even if the father was more of a threat, like in my house, and as sweet as my mother was, she ran the house. My dad taught us a good deal, but we could have turned out nearly as strong with just my mom's influence. Today, there's a lot of male absenteeism in our community, and women became the breadwinner and chief caretaker. Women are strong!

Of course, it's not going to happen overnight. I understand that many people will ignore it, as I've tried to ignore my own children's drug addiction. I believe that life circles around one rule: "If you don't take action on something, at least know how. You always have a choice to ignore it or do it, but you must know that you have a choice."

During the six months I volunteered at the rehab unit, I discovered that all of my learning had been a way to cope with my personal experiences. I wanted to understand what I failed to do as a parent to keep my children away from drugs. I wanted to understand why someone would take drugs. I wanted answers for all of the disappointment and heartache I felt over my own children.

As a volunteer, I clearly saw how these offenders didn't care and how their parents weren't holding them accountable.

I told the instructor, "You're not helpin' these people. You're aidin' their addiction."

That comment didn't go over too well, so I left before I made any enemies. I didn't feel as if I were contributing anything anyway. They did offer me a full-time job, paying $10 an hour to counsel. Some of my graduating classmates were making that amount, but I declined, mainly because the thought of getting to that building by 8 o'clock every morning didn't appeal to me!

Thoughts on Training

When I say that we should hold our children responsible, I'm not implying that I was a model parent in controlling my family with accountability and backing it with consequences. We will never find enough rules to conquer all human ills, but we do have the power to better our score by taking charge as a caregiver.

Modern day created many strong writings that I believe weaken a family, such as, "Children should have the right to challenge their parents' authority" or "You can't punish a child because it'll hurt their self-esteem." As Proverbs 22:6 teaches, "Train in the way he shall go." I believe that training is important to help younger minds believe they are somebody, not to control them. Training increases their hunger for knowledge and information.

I am very proud of my children. My oldest son, now retired, has been a sergeant and a California highway patrolman for over 33 years. My oldest daughter is a career worker for the San Francisco Giants and 49ers as a concession stand supervisor. My second daughter, now deceased, was an assistant counselor at the Weldon House Illicit Drugs Abuse Center. My second son, who was diagnosed at age nine with diabetes and who was active until his death at 38, was a serious singer with charisma! My third daughter's goal is to teach disabled children. She plans to enter state college this fall.

Push-Button Age

Most of us know which choices will make our lives easier, but we just don't want to do them. If you don't know the answer to something or you want an easier solution to a problem, you probably know someone (or someone who knows someone) whom you can trust to give you the answer. Life is like a math problem that we can't always solve by sitting in a room by ourselves. Our responsibility is to want the answer and go seek it.

Nowadays, we let computers do so much of the thinking. I call it the push-button age. If we want to figure out a math problem, we use a calculator. If we have a question about something, we look it up on our computer. We don't need to sit around and discuss things anymore; we can just tap on a computer for the answer. We let computers do our thinking instead of exercising our minds.

To survive, you have to learn to think for yourself. If you do everything I say, without giving it much thought, you cheat yourself. I believe that God gives us a mind so we can figure our problems and eventually figure out our unique calling. It's good to listen to other people but, in the end, you need to make your own decisions. You can't live your potential if you let someone or something else do the thinking for you.

Learning Opportunities

As I march through my senior years, looking forward to the land of no more, I reminisce about all of my experiences working under duress. It's clear to me now that all of my struggles made me strong by bringing out the best that resided innately in me. God creates all of us with such ability, but many don't want to push themselves enough to bring it out, so we waste our potential.

The funny thing about hindsight is the realization that mistakes you thought you made were actually learning opportunities to strengthen you in living a greater life.

I applaud going into business with my family without demanding commitments first. I applaud how my family passes on our history and teachings to our children and grandchildren in their homes and at large family meetings with extended family.

In our regular family meetings, we continued the concept of functional families by teaching young men to be responsible and young women to be respectful of themselves and others. We taught work ethics, financial management, and the concept that independence doesn't come to you as a gift—you must strive for it.

My brother, Caleb, started sponsoring this tradition in 1962 until his departure from this life. He was sitting with his head back on the sofa, talking to me, and his wife came home from work. Caleb greeted her, and then said, "There's some food in there if this boy didn't eat it all." His head dropped to the side and he was gone.

My brother, Isaiah, continued the family meetings after that; however, I haven't seen much enthusiasm over our family teachings or any happiness when we call everyone to a family meeting. The programs and idealism aren't convenient for many to hear as individuals or as a collective. Even in the community groups and outreach programs I volunteer for, people aren't listening with the same enthusiasm as they once did. I try to motivate groups to respect our community, register and vote, and become a part of building up their lives. In my teachings, I repeat a cherished saying that my mother used: "You don't live on earth and board in heaven." This means, you don't live your life here, just praying and thinking you'll end up in heaven. You need to earn your way up there through your actions down here.

A New Perspective

Throughout my life, I looked at my past and present wearing blinders. I only saw the struggle, the hard work, and the constant challenges. No matter how many goals I obtained, I couldn't remember much more than how hard I worked to get them. In my later years, I was able to see my whole life in perspective.

I kept this focus by seeing my life through a teaching I learned long ago: "Stay strong because nurturing people is like sowing seeds. Some come up and produce in various quantities, some get eaten by birds, and others don't come up at all."

When I evaluate my past with that teaching in my mind, I stir up boundless joy. I gratefully, freely, and joyfully sing the song that, through the years, the Lord has been good to me. Above all, He has and is still using me for His service.

I spent many years researching, reading, going to school, listening, watching, and thinking. Because of my pride, I wanted to make sure that my facts were correct when I spoke on a subject matter—not to show off, but to show that I wasn't ignorant. Now I see how that desire started from my early childhood days when I strove for self-acceptance. For me, though, this negative thinking of feeling insecure about myself didn't slow me down; instead, I used it as a building block to bring out my innate abilities.

I find joy in many of my trials and errors, marching through this challenging life with its perpetual changes. I find joy in how I opened some opportunities and closed others. As our Declaration of Independence tells us, we may not all arrive at the goal of our pursuits.

I say, "Take aim and shoot your best shot!"

As best as I could, I tried to follow the strong teachings from scripture. 2 Chronicles 15:6 says, "And nation was destroyed of nation, and city of city: for God did vex them with all adversity," and then 15:7, "Be ye strong therefore, and let not your hands be weak: for your work shall be rewarded." These verses tell us to do our best, know that we'll win some and lose some, and strive to be of service with sunshine in our demeanor. Thinking about all of the truly happy people I have met through the years, I see how the ones living with the most joy in their hearts were the most nonaggressive people I knew.

Value the Unorthodox

Scripture also tells us to criticize less and accept the unorthodox actions of others, such as 1 Timothy 5:19: "Against an elder receive not an accusation, but before two or three witnesses."

When I say "unorthodox actions," I especially think of my children and grandchildren. When they were on drugs, there were times when I was ready to tell them that I never wanted to see them again on this side of earth. Then, something told me to be patient and give them one more chance, which usually turned them around. That experience of hitting bottom and raising themselves back up proved more valuable than any lesson I could have taught.

With all the molding you do, remember to value what you mold. Trust and accept the lives people choose to live, no matter how difficult it is to bear. I spent my life trying to live up to my potential, and pushing my family and community to live up to theirs.

I put more value in those who lived busy, "important" lives, such as politicians and doctors, and I judged those who I thought were lazy and not maximizing their abilities. With all of the people whom I met over the years, the ones who seemed lackadaisical were often the ones who were of most value in the end. When you're down and need a helping hand, they're right by your side, whereas the other ones are too busy with their own lives to give you their time.

Watching my children and later grandchildren go through drug addiction helped me mature. They needed to experience the learning process themselves. I still attend some of the meetings where my children counsel their friends and others who are addicted. My children admit that they had no reason to be addicted, and they would make excuses for themselves with no basis to make them. It was their choice to get in and their choice to get out.

They tell others, "You are addicted because you make the *choice* to be addicted. Don't blame your parents or boyfriend or anyone but yourself. *You* are the one choosing to take the drugs."

I am grateful for being a husband to my girl Joan for 60 years now, a father, a grandfather, and a great-grandfather. At my age, it's easier to reminisce over the good days, see some of the joys I didn't appreciate back then, accept the sorrows, and forgive the many bad days.

I see the times when I wanted to throw in the towel and applaud myself for holding on. I am grateful for what I achieved as a result. Each of these memories combine into the momentous knowledge that I was—and still am—here through the visible help from the good and merciful God.

I am thankful to God that I am active, mobile, and cognitive. As I sojourn to the close of my life, I have no sad thoughts because I am saved!How do I know? I believe what God says in Romans 10:9, "That if thou shalt confess with thy mouth the Lord Jesus, and shalt believe in thine heart that God hath raised him from the dead, thou shalt be saved."

Consider that as a present to the end of this book.

Made in the USA
San Bernardino, CA
13 September 2014